Facts On File
NATIONAL PROFILES

Japan

FACTS ON FILE
NATIONAL
PROFILES

Japan

GEORGE THOMAS KURIAN

FactsOnFile
New York • Oxford • Sydney

Facts On File National Profiles: Japan

Facts On File, Inc.
460 Park Avenue South
New York, NY 10016
USA

Facts On File Limited
Collins Street
Oxford OX4 1XJ
United Kingdom

Facts On File Pty Ltd
Talavera & Khartoum Rds
North Ryde NSW 2113
Australia

Library of Congress Cataloging-in-Publication Data

Kurian, George Thomas.
    Facts On File national profiles. Japan/George Thomas Kurian.
        p.   cm.
    Includes bibliographical references.

        1. Japan.   I. Title.   II. Title: Japan.
    DS806.K845   1989
    952—dc20   89-23781

ISBN 0-8160-2265-8

British and Australian CIP data available on request from Facts On File.

Facts On File books are available at special discounts when purchased in bulk
quantities for businesses, associations, institutions or sales promotions. Please
contact the Special Sales Department of our New York office at 212/683-2244
(dial 800/322-8755 except in NY, AK or HI).

Composition by Logidec
Manufactured by R.R. Donnelley & Sons, Inc.
Printed in the United States of America

10 9 8 7 6 5 4 3 2 1

This book is printed on acid-free paper.

CONTENTS

INTRODUCTION

Japan, part of an ongoing series of national profiles derived from the larger Encyclopedias of the First, Second, and Third Worlds, is a survey of contemporary Japan, examining its potential and performance in 32 key sectors and describing the evolution and growth of its major institutions.

In 1962 when Herman Kahn of the Hudson Institute predicted that Japan will become a superpower and "the most productive economy the world has ever known" by 2000 and that the 21st century will be the Japanese century, he was greeted with a shrug of disbelief and a cry of *absit omen*. Yet, barely a quarter of a century later, the prediction is close to fulfillment and his forecasts have acquired the ominous ring and vatic certainty of a Delphic oracle.

As the world's only non-Western superpower and the world's first unarmed superpower, Japan has presented an enigma to Western observers. Without any of the traditional resources or bases of power — no missiles, no raw materials, no colonies — Japan has made itself into a factory and trading house for the entire world. Every year its economic growth rate has exceeded the forecasts of its own and Western economists, forcing them to examine the mystique of its success and seek a clue to the seemingly endless economic miracle. In fact, the Japanese economy has been intensively studied from every angle in recent years and more books have been published on it than on that of any other major world power.

In the 1950s the Japanese economy doubled in size, going from small to medium. This in itself was called an economic miracle but it was neither spectacular nor unprecedented. Many nations in Europe had done the same. In the 1960s the economy grew by a factor of three, going from medium to large. In the process it passed those of the United Kingdom, France and West Germany to become the world's third largest economy. By 1988, its GNP was half that of the United States and grazing that of the Soviet Union, and its per capita GNP had surpassed that of the United States. If it can maintain its growth rate in the last decade of the 20th century, Japan will surpass the United States in aggregate GNP by 2000 — and thus will have the world's most powerful economy.

The dimensions and indicators of the Japanese economy are among the most closely watched data in the world. Japan is the second largest industrial producer in the world, with a gross output in 1986 of $395.148 billion, half that of the United States, but double that of West Germany and four times that of the United Kingdom. Not only is it the second largest trading nation, with exports of $210.553 billion and imports of $127.553 billion, but it was, even before the 1986 devaluation of the yen, the most profitable trading nation, with an annual trade surplus over $75 billion. At 11.5% its annual export growth rate during 1980-86 was the highest of any nation, and its terms of trade in 1986 (with 1980 = 100) was 156 compared to an average of 109 for all industrial nations. The composition of its trade is even more startling. In their bilateral trade, the United States exports mostly agricultural goods to Japan while Japan exports mostly manufactured goods, thus placing the United States in the category of an agricultural colony of Japan. Japan is the largest creditor nation in the world and its foreign investments are so large and their growth so fast that even MITI figures are outdated by the time they are published. Its gross investments around the world will soon approach $1 trillion and its investments in the United States are exceeded only by those of the United Kingdom. When the first edition of the *New Book of World Rankings* was published in 1979 Japan appeared in first place in only one ranking — shipbuilding. By 1989 Japan ranked first in over 17 industrial rankings and its industrial leadership is diverse and versatile, covering not only autos, steel, ships, television, radios, cameras, optical instruments and machine tools but also pianos, motorcycles, art pottery, cultured pearls and even zippers. It is fast moving to take over supercomputers, robotics and artificial intelligence, very large integrated circuits, superconductors and other frontier technologies. The world's top banks, advertising firms and securities traders are all Japanese. While steel production is failing in all major industrial countries, Japan, with 14 of the world's 22 large blast furnaces, is expanding its output. In terms of corporate assets, Japanese predominance is even more frightening. For example, the assets of Nippon Telephone and Telegraph exceed the combined assets of General Motors, IBM, General Electric and AT&T.

In starting off the ground in the 1950s, the Japanese were able to buy sophisticated technology from the West at bargain basement rates. The Japanese also were ruthless in getting rid of their inefficient industries. Early in its career Japan divided its industries into four groups: Throwaway Industries, in which Japan did not wish to compete; Early Stage Industries, in which Japan had only a slight competitive advantage; Second Stage Industries, in which Japan excelled in the 1960s and 1970s and in which it soon built up a monopoly; and Third Stage Industries, in which Japan hopes to build the foundations of its industrial might.

Throwaway Industries	Early Stage Industries	Second Stage Industries	Third Stage Industries
Coal	Cotton textiles	Iron, steel	Automobiles
Nonferrous	Sewing machines	Shipbuilding	Precision tools
Paper, pulp	Bicycles	Trucks	Large construct-
Agricultural	Pottery	Television	ion equipment
		Radio	Computer elec-
		Rail, rolling	tronics
		stock	Robotics

Japan displayed considerable flexibility in moving from one group to another as soon as competition threatened its dominance. The Japanese also sought the commanding heights and the most prestigious technologies in each sector. It took Japan about 20 years to move from stage 2 to stage 3 but less than half that time to move from stage 3 to stage 4.

Herman Kahn summarizes several reasons or favorable conditions that contributed to rapid Japanese growth rates:

1. High savings and investment rates, about twice those of the United States
2. Superior education and training
3. Adequate capitalization
4. Readily available risk capital
5. Technological genius
6. High morale and commitment to growth
7. Achievement and work-oriented employees
8. Willingness to make necessary adjustments and sacrifices
9. Excellent market direction and management
10. Adquate access to world resources
11. Relatively few pressures to divert resources to low economic uses
12. Many byproducts of a high momentum of economic growth
13. Less than 1% allotted to national defense
14. Willingess to abandon weak or obsolete industries

Exogenous factors include the presence of a rich and exposed U.S. market as a milch cow, developments in ocean transport that made Japan's lack of natural resources less of a disadvantage than it would have been 50 years ago, and the easy exploitation of the Third World.

Japan's industrial preeminence has not been achieved at the cost of the environment or quality of life. Japanese pollution standards are among the toughest in the world. Japan's average life expectancy is higher than that of the United States and is rapidly approaching that of Scandinavian countries. Japan also has the lowest infant mortality rate in the world. While the incidence of crime has risen in every modern developed society along with the standard of living, it has declined in Japan. Japanese cities are believed to be among the safest in the world both night and day.

But the Japanese success cannot be explained solely through economic factors. A good part of the explanation lies in what may be summed up in the word "character." The Japanese are a disciplined and group-minded people capable of extraordinary efforts in the pursuit of the common good. It has been said that Japan is the last "Calvinist" nation on earth where the work ethic still survives. A further clue lies in the symbiosis of business and nation. To adapt Calvin Coolidge's famous dictum on U.S. business, "The business of Japan is business." Conversely, the business of Japanese business is Japan. Japanese tend to identify the success of a business firm with the success of the nation and view business with the same kind of single-minded frenzy that the British display toward soccer. When it comes to Japan against the rest of the world, even trade competitors share their secrets and pool their resources. Corporate culture is not considered alien to the national culture as in the West but is considered as one and the same. In the words of *Newsweek*, "The country is not merely Japan, but Japan, Inc." In a nation where watching the gross national product is a gross national pastime, trade representatives and bank managers are folk heroes. When the *shosha in*, as these heroes are known, depart from Tokyo's Haneda Airport on their forays, they are given a hero's farewell with shouts of *banzai* and their exploits are celebrated on their return with the same kind of admiration that is accorded astronauts on their return to earth.

Japan's national society is thus unique and distinctive. The feeling of national distinctiveness has been strengthened over the centuries despite massive borrowings from other cultures. Nation, race, language and culture are enmeshed in a tightly threaded fabric that cannot be separated. Race and culture loom large in Japanese thinking. Insularity is a matter of pride with the Japanese, referred to as *shimaguni-konjo* — the feelings of an island people.

The Japanese also have an extraordinary talent for narrowing national energies into well defined tasks and objectives. It is a conscious democracy where it is in bad taste for the majority to outvote the minority without concessions. The word *manjo-ichi* (unanimity) has a magical ring in Japanese thought. Although they wax indignant occasionally over public problems, they — like the British — have an extraordinary capacity to endure discomfort and inconveniences that would enrage or provoke other peoples. It is a society imbued with a sense of hierarchic order. In fact, there is no Japanese word that expresses the Western concept of equal, as in all men are equal. As a corollary, the Japanese traditionally think of themselves as members of a group and their satisfactions come largely through group fulfillment of group objectives. Unlike in the West where interpersonal relationships are fluid, the whole gamut of obligational relationships in Japan is expressed in a few anchor concepts, the most important of which are *ringi* (consensus), *giri* (duty), *on* (obligation), *ninjo* (feelings), *kokutai* (patriotism, or the mystic sense of being part of a special and distinct national polity) and *tenko* (transformation and restoration).

The last remaining foundation of Japanese success is education. Among the large countries of the world, only the Soviet Union and the United States compare with Japan in the percentage of population with post-secondary education. The Japanese system is even better than that of these two countries. On the basis of objective tests, the Japanese appear to have achieved American mass education combined with European quality. Further, Japanese students generally surpass their counterparts in the West in mathematics and science.

However, Japan is not exempt from the problems that rapid success brings in its train. Although it is now the most international of all major powers, its power is indeed very fragile. Japan is much admired but not widely trusted or liked. The country's narrow emphasis on economic growth has precluded a broader base of political influence. In fact, its political influence is so inconsequential in world affairs that it has been described as an economic giant but a political pygmy. Even within Japan, ordinary citizens are more interested in social benefits than economic growth, and the new generation reared in affluence has little interest in economic growth at all. Detractors are quick to point out that the growth rate has already shown signs of stress. The once lively domestic market is now satiated and the world markets — the mainstay of Japanese exports — are becoming rapidly saturated. Korea, Taiwan and other Newly Industrializing Countries with lower labor costs and newer plants will be able to undersell Japan in world markets in a broad range of products and cash in on the same competitive advantage that Japan once had. Japan will therefore have to give up many of its labor-intensive industries to those countries and move into the high-technology areas in a head-on collision course with the West and into service areas where Japan enjoys fewer competitive advantages.

Companies are heavily indebted to banks. When growth rates were high they could easily repay loans. With a system of permanent employment, companies also are stuck with a highly paid older work force. With less room for expansion they do not often have work for everyone and disguised unemployment is growing. The proportion of older persons in the population is expected to reach European levels by 2000 when the nation will be confronted with a smaller work force, a larger welfare bill and increasing tax burdens. The social consequences of such a situation also cause concern to the leadership. Social cleavages will become more prominent and the broad-based consensus on which the nation depends for its stability will no longer be a viable phenomenon.

Until now, Japan could selectively control imports of foreign ideas and customs and maintain the phalanx of national solidarity. With increasing foreign contact and internationalization, Japan will find it hard to control the flow of foreign influences and to preserve the distinctive features of Japanese society. During growth the grand vision of a triumphant Japan surpassing its Western rivals gave the entire society a sense of purpose. The vision achieved, Japan has no longer a clear direction.

At the same time, Japan has a resilience that has astounded its critics. The fact is that Japan is likely to remain extraordinarily competitive in world markets for at least another century. It has the cohesion and leadership to maintain an effective postindustrial society without suffering any debilitating social changes. Its commanding lead in the new technologies will enable it to maintain and even increase its virtual stranglehold over the global economy. Already Japan is the information capital of the world and its six largest trading companies are superior to any foreign company in their ability to convert information into economic power. Interest rates are now far lower than during the rapid growth years. The large manufacturers are helping to modernize the medium-level companies where Japan had been weak until now. Further, the heavy Japanese investments overseas in the 1980s will begin to pay off within the next decade, providing the nation with a security blanket against domestic failures. Huge, integrated Japanese-led construction projects are springing up in all parts of the world, providing an outlet for Japanese production without attracting charges of dumping that the export of consumer products generally do.

Japan is part of an ongoing series of National Profiles of which Kate Kelly is the editor. To her and Bill Drennan, a truly remarkable copyeditor, I owe a deep debt of gratitude. I would also like to acknowledge, as always, the help and encouragement of Edward W. Knappman, publisher.

George Thomas Kurian
Yorktown Heights

JAPAN

JAPAN

BASIC FACT SHEET

OFFICIAL NAME: Japan (Nippon)

ABBREVIATION: JA

CAPITAL: Tokyo

HEAD OF STATE: Emperor Akihito (from 1989)

HEAD OF GOVERNMENT: Prime Minister Toshiki Kaifu (from 1989)

NATURE OF GOVERNMENT: Constitutional monarchy

POPULATION: 122,626,038 (1988)

AREA: 377,483 sq. km. (145,747 sq. mi.)

MAJOR ETHNIC GROUPS: Japanese

LANGUAGE: Japanese

RELIGIONS: Shintoism; Buddhism; Christianity; also new religions

UNIT OF CURRENCY: Yen

NATIONAL FLAG: Sun flag (Hi-no-Maru) consists of a red circle on a white background

NATIONAL EMBLEM: A single round gold chrysanthemum with 16 symmetrical petals

NATIONAL ANTHEM: "Kimigayo" (The Reign of Our Emperor)

NATIONAL HOLIDAYS: Emperor's Birthday (April 29); Culture Day (November 3); Health-Sports Day (October 10); Autumnal Equinox Day (September 23 or 24); Respect for the Aged Day (September 15); Children's Day (May 5); Constitution Day (May 3); Vernal Equinox Day (March 21 or 22); Commemoration of the Founding of the Nation Day (February 11); Adults' Day (January 15).

NATIONAL CALENDAR: Gregorian

PHYSICAL QUALITY OF LIFE INDEX: 99 (on an ascending scale with 100 as the maximum)

DATE OF INDEPENDENCE: c. 660 B.C.

DATE OF CONSTITUTION: May 3, 1947

WEIGHTS & MEASURES: Metric

GEOGRAPHICAL FEATURES

The Japanese archipelago forms a convex crescent off the eastern coast of the Asian mainland, bounded on the north by the Sea of Okhotsk, on the east and south by the Pacific Ocean, on the southwest by the East China Sea and on the west by the Sea of Japan. The total area of Japan is 377,483 sq. km. (145,747 sq. mi.), extending 3,008 km. (1,869 mi.) northeast to southwest and 1,645 km. (1,022 mi.) southeast to northwest. Its total coastline is 9,387 km. (5,833 mi.). No point in Japan is more than 150 km. (93 mi.) from the sea. The distance between Japan and the Asian mainland, of which the nearest point is the Korean Peninsula, is about 200 km. (124 mi.).

The country consists of four principal islands—Hokkaido, Honshu, Shikoku, and Kyushu; over 3,000 small adjacent islands and islets, including Oshima in the Nanpo chain; and over 200 other, smaller islands, including those of the Amami, Okinawa and Sakishima chains of the Ryukyu Islands archipelago. The national territory also includes the small Bonin (Ogasawara) Islands, Iwo Jima and the Volcano Islands in the Pacific Ocean some 1,100 km. (684 mi.) south of central Honshu. A territorial dispute with the Soviet Union concerns the two southernmost of the Kuril Islands, Etorofu and Kunashiri , and the smaller Shikotan and Habomai islands group northeast of Hokkaido. The four major islands are separated only by narrow straits and form a natural entity.

The capital is Tokyo, formerly known as Edo, on the northwestern shore of the Bay of Tokyo in southeastern Honshu. In 1988 it was the largest metropolitan center in the world, with a population spilling over into the Yokohoma region, with which it constitutes the Kanto region. There are 10 other cities with a population of over 1 million and four with populations of over 2 million. Some of them have had phenomenal growth since the turn of the century. In 1859 Yokohama was a fishing village with a population of only 350. Osaka, on the northeastern shore of Osaka Bay, is one of the imperial cities (or *fu*) and it has the greatest port in the country, though with an entirely artificial harbor. Nagoya, capital of the Aichi prefecture, is the center of the third-ranking industrial area in Japan. Sapporo is the most important city on the island of Hokkaido. Kyoto, the most important inland city, was the residence of the mikado (emperor) until 1869 and the historic capital of Japan. It is noted for its celebrated Kyomidzu Buddhist pagoda. Kobe, a deep-water port west of Osaka, was built up at first with British and American capital and grew by absorbing the old city of Hyogo.

PRINCIPAL CITIES*
(Population in 1986)

Tokyo (capital)†	8,354,615	Oita	390,096
Yokohama	2,992,926	Takatsuki	384,784
Osaka	2,636,249	Hirakata	382,253
Nagoya	2,116,381	Urawa	377,235
Sapporo	1,542,979	Omiya	373,022
Kyoto	1,479,218	Asahikawa	363,631
Kobe	1,410,834	Fukuyama	360,261
Fukuoka	1,160,440	Iwaki	350,569
Kawasaki	1,088,624	Suita	348,948
Kitakyushu	1,056,402	Nagano	336,973
Hiroshima	1,044,118	Fujisawa	328,387

PRINCIPAL CITIES* (continued)

Sakai	818,271	Nara	327,702
Chiba	788,930	Takamatsu	326,994
Sendai	700,254	Toyohashi	322,142
Okayama	572,479	Machida	321,188
Kumamoto	555,719	Hakodate	319,194
Kagoshima	530,502	Toyama	314,111
Higashiosaka	522,805	Kochi	312,241
Hamamatsu	514,118	Toyoda	308,111
Amagasaki	509,115	Naha	303,674
Funabashi	506,966	Koriyama	301,673
Sagamihara	482,778	Akita	296,400
Niigata	475,630	Aomori	294,045
Shizuoka	468,362	Kawagoe	285,437
Himeji	452,917	Okazaki	284,996
Nagasaki	449,382	Miyazaki	279,114
Kanazawa	430,481	Maebashi	277,319
Matsudo	427,473	Yao	276,394
Yokosuka	427,116	Tokorozawa	275,168
Matsuyama	426,658	Kashiwa	273,128
Hachioji	426,654	Fukushima	270,762
Nishinomiya	421,267	Shimonoseki	269,169
Kurashiki	413,632	Akashi	263,363
Toyonaka	413,213	Yokkaichi	263,001
Gifu	411,743	Neyagawa	258,228
Utsunomiya	405,375	Tokushima	257,884
Kawaguchi	403,015	Ichinomiya	257,388
Wakayama	401,352	Kasugai	256,990
Ichikawa	397,822	Koshigaya	253,479

*Except for Tokyo, the data for each city refer to an urban county (shi), an administrative division that may include some scattered or rural population as well as an urban center.

†The figure refers to the 23 wards (ku) of Tokyo. The population of Tokyo-to (Tokyo Prefecture) was 11,829,363.

The Japanese islands are essentially the summits of mountain ridges that have been uplifted near the outer edge of the Asian continental shelf. Consequently the country is extremely mountainous, and the plains and intermontane basins scattered throughout make up only 25% of the national territory. A long series of mountain ranges runs down the middle of the archipelago, dividing it in half—the "face" fronting the Pacific Ocean and the "back" facing the Sea of Japan. Although the mountains are precipitous, most of them are only a few hundred meters high and present a somewhat monotonous profile. Central Japan, however, is marked by the convergence of three mountain chains that form the Japanese Alps (Hida Mountains), which extend from north to south for 97 to 113 km. (60 to 70 mi.), with about 15 peaks that exceed 3,048 m. (10,000 ft.). The highest point in the country is Mount Fuji, a dormant volcano that rises to

3,776 m. (12,389 ft). Snow lingers here late into spring and the mountainsides are streaked by fallen rocks, but there are no true glaciers.

Japanese plains, unlike those of Europe, are not basins of sedimentary deposits but depressed zones in which great masses of alluvium have accumulated. They have a fairly level profile, sloping rather steeply to the sea, where they end in a line of dunes. Most of the plains are along the coast, including the largest, Kanto, where Tokyo is located; Nobi, surrounding Nagoya; Kinki, in the Osaka-Kyoto area; Sendai, in northeastern Honshu; and Ishikarai and Tokachi, on Hokkaido. Wide riverbeds lined by high banks cut across these lowlands. Ascending terraces are a familiar feature of the interfluvial areas. On the approaches to the mountains, the slopes steepen and are laced by numerous watercourses, sometimes isolating a group of hills. Many plains are found in the interior, particularly in the mountainous region of central Honshu known as Tosan, where enclosed basins (such as Kofu, Nagano, Lake Suwa and Matsumoto) are joined by valleys.

Japan has a 9,387 km. (5,833 mi.) coastline, representing 1,6 km. (1 mi.) for every 13 sq. km. (5 sq mi.) of land area, a ratio equal to that of Great Britain. The shores are of tectonic origin, which explains why the pattern is different on the Sea of Japan and the Pacific coasts. Along the latter, the fracture cuts obliquely across the shoreline, forming large indentations such as the Bozo, Izu, and Kii peninsulas and the bays of Sendai, Tokyo and Ise (Nagoya). The deep trough that contains the Inland Sea and the two openings at either end also have been bent perpendicularly, which accounts for the violin shape of the island of Shikoku and the bulge at the center of the body of water. In contrast, the shore is less indented on the Sea of Japan side. The entire southwestern coast of Kyushu, from Kagoshima Bay to the Straits of Shimonoseki, is deeply fragmented and fractured. The northern half of the coastline is uplifted from the sea, while the southern half has subsided and been invaded by the sea. Flat shores terminating in dunes are common along the Sea of Japan. On the Pacific side, flat shores are found at the head of the principal bays, where the great metropolises are situated. North of Tokyo Bay is a type of landscape called *suigo* (land of water). Here the plain is exactly at mean sea level, protected by levees and locks and by a system of pumps, as in the Netherlands.

Topographically Japan is divided into eight major regions, of which the islands of Hokkaido, Shikoku and Kyushu each form a region, and the island of Honshu forms five. Hokkaido constitutes more than one-fifth of Japan. It was long looked upon as a remote frontier area because of its forests and rugged climate. Hokkaido is divided along a line extending from Cape Soya to Cape Erimo. The eastern half includes the Daisetsu Mountains, at the foot of which lie the plains of Tokachi and Konsen. This is the most inhospitable section of the country. The western half is milder and less hilly.

The Tohoku (literally, Northeast) occupies the northeastern part of Honshu above approximately the 37th parallel. It is a dry, bright region with flat, well-drained alluvial plains. The region still is considered a rural backcountry where traditional dialects and customs persist.

The central zone, corresponding to the widest parts of the archipelago, consists of the Kanto, Chubu, and Chugoku regions. Kanto is the most industrialized region in Japan and includes the Tokyo-Yokohama industrial complex. The Chubu region, lying west of the Kanto, is characterized by the greater height and ruggedness of its mountains. It comprises three distinct districts: Hokuriku, a coastal strip on the Sea of Japan; Tosan, the central highlands; and Tokai, a narrow corridor lying along the Pacific coast. Hokoriku is the "snow country" so dear to Japanese romanticism, where the winters are swept by violent squalls and the summers are hot and humid. It rains year-round. The Tosan, often called the Roof of Japan, includes the Japanese Alps. The population is chiefly concentrated in six elevated basins connected by narrow valleys. The western part of the Tokai district includes the Nobi Plain. The Kinki region lies to the west and consists of a comparatively narrow area of Honshu stretching from the Sea of Japan on the north to the Pacific Ocean on the south. It includes Japan's second-largest commercial-industrial complex, centered in Osaka and Kobe, and the two former imperial cities of Nara and Kyoto, The other imortant lowland area of Kinki, the Osaka Plain, forms the Harshin commercial industrial complex. The Chugoku region occupies the western end of Honshu and is divided into two distinct districts by mountains running through the central part. The northern, somewhat narrower, part is known as San'in, (shady side) and the southern part as San'yo (sunny side).

The Shikoku region also is divided by mountains into a narrow northern subregion that fronts the Inland Sea and a wider southern part that faces the Pacific Ocean. Most of the population lives in the northern zone. The southern part is mostly mountainous and sparsely populated.

Kyushu, the southernmost of the main islands, is divided into northern and southern parts by the Kyushu Mountains, which run diagonally across the middle of the island. The northern part is one of Japan's most industrialized regions and includes the Kitakyushu industrial region.

The Ryukyu Islands include well over 200 islands and islets, of which fewer than half are populated. They extend in a chain generally southwestward from Tokara Strait to within 193 km. (120 mi.) of Taiwan.

A tenth of the world's volcanoes are in Japan. Of the 265 known volcanoes in Japan, 20 have been active since the beginning of the century. They are particularly numerous in Hokkaido, the Fossa Magna and Kyushu. The mountainous area of Kyushu resembles a lunar landscape, with wide craters and cones of every form, ranging from the ash cone of Mount Fuji to the volcanic dome of Daisetsu. Volcanic eruptions cause few deaths because they can be anticipated. Among the great eruptions in modern times were those of Mount Bandai in 1888 and Mount Aso in 1953 and 1958.

Japan also is subject to periodic earthquakes, with over 1,500 recorded annually. Minor tremors occur almost daily in one part of the country or another, causing a slight shaking of buildings. Major earthquakes, although rarer, can result in thousands of deaths, as in the Kanto earthquake of 1923, in which 130,000 were killed. There are three particularly sensitive seismic zones: the Bozo Peninsula, less than 56 km. (35 mi.) from Tokyo; the Sea of Japan, some 105 km. (65 mi.) north of Osaka; and the Pacific coast in northern Tohoku and Hokkaido. Because of the danger they pose, Japan has become a world leader in research on causes and prediction of earthquakes and the construction of earthquakeproof buildings. Extensive civil defense efforts focus on training in protection against earthquakes, in particular against accompanying fires, which represent a greater danger. Undersea earthquakes also expose the Japanese coastline to danger from tsunamis. An equally great hazard consists of movements of the earth that shake loose entire mountainsides. These landslides, generally composed of clay, may be from 6 to 23 m. (20 to 75 ft.) deep, several hundred feet wide and up to 4 km. (2.5 mi.) long. The speed of the flow varies with the season and the water content of the soil. Landslides are especially numerous on Hokuriku on the Sea of Japan side, where more than 10,000 have been counted in recorded history. The largest sometimes carry with them entire paddy fields, tree groves and even houses. This makes it necessary for the communities affected to redistribute the land periodically, as the property at the tip of the flow steadily shrinks in size.

At the head of most of the bays where the great cities are located, the land is sinking slowly, causing buildings to subside up to 38 mm. (1.5 in.) annually. Roads and water mains also are affected. Since 1935 the port area of Osaka has subsided almost 3 m. (10 ft.).

Japan is perhaps the only country in the world to suffer from both typhoons and snow. Typhoons cause an average of 1,500 deaths and destroy 20,000 dwellings a year. Southern Shikoku is particularly vulnerable. In regions bordering the Sea of Japan, winter monsoons, laden with snow, can be as destructive as typhoons. Snowfall is heavy along the western coast, where it covers the ground for almost four months a year, depositing a very thick blanket on the streets and rooftops. The cost of keeping railway tracks and roads open is a heavy burden on the municipalities.

Although the country is exceptionally well watered, the absence of large plains has precluded the formation of a good river system. The longest river, the Tone River, is only 322 km. (200 mi.) long. Rivers tend to be steep and swift and hence unsuitable for navigation. Moreover, the mountainous terrain and the absence of glaciers make the flow highly irregular. The early summer "plum rains" account for a large part of the annual precipitation and turn slow streams into raging torrents. In winter these riverbeds are transformed into wide stretches of gravel furrowed by thin trickles of water. The peak rainy season is from May to October, with regional variations. Rivers are used mostly for hydroelectric production and for irrigation.

The landscape is speckled with lakes of every description and size. The biggest is Biwa, 674 sq. km. (260 sq. mi.) in area, which fills a large fault basin east of Kyoto. Celebrated in song and legend, Biwa is threatened today by pollution as well as the demands for fresh water from Osaka (connected to Biwa by the Yodo River, its outlet) and Kyoto (connected by a tunnel).

Floods are common, especially in the Pacific coastal areas, where the subsidence of land makes it necessary to raise large embankments and dikes against rivers that flow at a level well above that of the surrounding plains. During periods of heavy rains angry waters bearing great masses of alluvium break through the embankments, inundating the adjacent fields and covering them with a thick carpet of gravel and sand. Sometimes typhoons bringing fresh torrents of water to the rivers convert whole plains into vast lakes and sweep away roads and railways.

CLIMATE & WEATHER

For a country of its size, Japan has a surprising variety of climatic conditions. Its climatic range often is compared to that of the eastern coast of North America from Nova Scotia to Georgia. Tokyo is at the same general latitude as Athens, Tehran and San Francisco. In general, the Japanese climate is humid and temperate, with marked seasonal variations justly celebrated in art and literature. The two primary influences are Japan's location off the Asian mainland and its latitudinal extent, stretching from the shores of Soviet Primorsk to the tropical regions of Okinawa. It also is open to the major oceanic currents. In addition, there are great differences in altitude, sometimes within relatively short distances. Climate further varies with the location, on the Pacific or on the Sea of Japan.

The climate is of two major types: marine and continental. The former is regulated by two ocean currents: The Kuroshio Current (Black Current) flows northward on the Pacific side and warms areas as far north as Tokyo. A small branch, the Tsushima Current, flows up the Sea of Japan side. The Oyashio

Current (Parent Current) is a cold-water current from the North that descends along the eastern coast of Hokkaido and Tohoku. The meeting point of these currents is a bountiful fishing ground.

The mainland Asian climate regulates temperatures and precipitation. In the cold season Siberia is the home of an anticyclone, while the Aleutian area is a zone of depression. Situated exactly between these two centers, Japan is swept by a north-to-south current of air that is cool and dry in the beginning but becomes variable and humid after its passage over the Sea of Japan. Other disturbances at the southern edge of this current result in turbulence throughout the air mass. When the air current reaches the archipelago and the warm waters of the Kuroshio Current, it becomes laden with water, which it then proceeds to discharge in the form of heavy snowfalls. In the summer the situation is reversed. Mainland Asia becomes a low-pressure area, while high subtropical pressures advance toward the Okhotsk Sea. The prevailing south-to-north winds are slow-moving and irregular because of their saturation. From the Okhotsk Sea the air moves southwest, forming a front upon contact with the tropical and equatorial maritime air from the south. Two periods of heavy rains result, one in June called the "plum rains" and the other in September. Between these two periods, the archipelago is hot, humid and rainless. From the end of summer through October, still more violent atmospheric disturbances occur, resulting in typhoons. Most typhoons follow the paths taken by the two branches of the Kuroshio Current, whose surface temperature is at its peak at this season.

The seasonal temperatures in Japan are lower than those at similar latitudes on the Asian mainland due to the country's insularity. Especially in winter, temperatures are several degrees lower than those in Europe because of the cold winds from the mainland, which prevail for four months of the year. In Hokkaido a minimum of -40°C (-40°F) was recorded at Asahikawa, while the annual average for Sapporo is only 6.8°C (44°F). Hakodate has -2.9°C (27°F) in January and 22.2°C (72°F) in July. The average in Tokyo in January is 2.4°C (36°F). Even the most southerly regions of Japan have several weeks of frost each year. In Shikoku and Kyushu summer is the dominant season because of its duration. In general, summer heat and humidity vary little from one end of the country to the other. The July average is 26°C (79°F) in Kagoshima in the South and 22°C (72°F) in Sapporo in the North.

Japan has two well-watered zones: one between Kanazawa and Niigata on Sea of Japan coast, and between the Kii Peninsula and Kyushu on the Pacific coast. On the Pacific side it rains only during summer, but the precipitation is greater than on the opposite coast. In Kochi 1,626 mm. (64 in.) have been recorded between May and September. Between these two regions lie the dry inland regions, where droughts are common. The central basin of the Inland Sea receives barely 610 mm. (24 in.) between May and September. While the winters are hard on the Sea of Japan coast, on the Pacific side the sky is clear and the air brisk, although stirred at times by icy gusts. Tokyo in January has one and one-half times the sunshine of Rome.

The cycle of seasons thus is quite distinct for each region. The main difference is the drop in temperature from the Southwest to the Northeast. The difference is illustrated by the dates on which cherry trees bloom, marking the advent of spring: March 25 in Kyushu; April 10 in Kansai and south Hokuriku: April 20 in Tokyo; April 30 in northern Tohoku; and May 10 in Hakodate, in southern Hokkaido. The number of days per year on which the country is free of ice also varies with the regions, from 260 days on the westernmost tip of Kyushu to 240 along the Pacific coast from Nagoya to Tokyo, 200 at Sendai, 180 at the northern extremity of Honshu and 150 in central Hokkaido. Thus summers and winters vary in length on the four islands. Summer lasts for four months in the central region, for three months in Tohoku and Hokkaido and five months in the subtropical regions of Shikoku and Kyushu. Even though the duration varies, summers tend to be hot and humid in all regions. Even the Far North experiences the kind of tropical weather that prevails in the southwest for most of summer.

POPULATION

The population of Japan in 1988 was 122,636,038, based on the last census, held in 1985, when the population was 121,047,196. Japan ranks seventh in the world in size of population and 56th in the world in land area. The population is expected to reach 124,275,000 by 1990 and 132,589,000 by 2000.

Two aspects of the country's population are likely to exert significant influence on future social and demographic trends. The first is density, and the second is age structure. The average density is 323 persons per sq. km. (837 persons per sq. mi.), a figure exceeded only by the Netherlands/Belgium and Bangladesh. The actual density is much higher on the basis of significant criteria. To begin with, only the plains are occupied, and per sq. km. of agricultural land, the density rises to over 1,930 (over 5,000 per sq. mi.). In settled areas such as the Kanto Plain, the densities are even higher. The highest concentrations of population are found in Kanto, Kansai, Tokai, Chugoku and the northeastern quarter of Kyushu.

The second problematic aspect of the population is its age structure. As the death rates declined steadily, from 15 per 1,000 in 1945 to 6.2 per 1,000 in 1988, life expectancy climbed to among the highest in the world. The average life span is expected to reach 75.07 years for males and 80.41 years for females in 2050, after which it is expected to level off. Lower death rates combined with lower birth rates and higher life expectancy have resulted in an aging of the population. The proportion of the elderly in the population is expected to reach 15.6% in 2000, rising further to 18.8% in 2010 and to 22.2% in 2043. Thereafter the upward trend is expected to slow as a result of increased birth rates and to stabilize to about 19% to 20% by 2075. The percentage of young persons (below 15) always has surpassed that of the elderly in this century in Japan, but in 2009 the ratio will be reversed, with the elderly constituting 18.7% and the young 18.4%. This situation will prevail until 2059. The proportion of the productive-age population (ages 15–64) will have grown from 67.4% in 1980 to 70.0% in 1990 but will decrease thereafter, to 61.5% in 2025 and to 59.3% in 2040. In ratio of aged population both to total population and to the young, Japan ranks among the top five nations of the world. The Dependent Population Index (the ratio of minors and the elderly to the productive-age population) is expected to rise from 42.8 in 1990 to 68.6 in 2040. It will then gradually decline to 61 by 2080. All these changes in the age composition of the population are reflected in the age pyramid, which was bell-shaped until the 1980s, but it is expected to change to a jar shape by 2000 and to a rough rectangle by 2020.

Japan's birth rate remained relatively low until the second half of the 19th century. The 1872 population census recorded a population of only 34.8 million, a level that had been maintained for the previous 150 years. Thereafter until World War II, natural increase led to a virtual doubling of the population. In 1950 the population passed 83 million, in 1970 it passed 100 million and in 1975 it passed 110 million. As a result of declining fertility combined with late marriages, the birth rate per 1,000 is expected to fluctuate in the 10 to 14 band until 2080. Because of a lowering mortality rate (reflecting the aging of the population), natural increase will be slower and will fall below, the zero level from 2010. It will not start rising again until after 2075.

Urbanization was not a major factor in Japanese demography until the end of World War II. By 1960 a total of 63.5% of the population was living in cities; by 1986 the total had risen to 76%. The Japanese divide their human settlements into villages (mura) and towns (cho) of between 5,000 and 30,000 inhabitants and cities (shi) of over 30,000 inhabitants. The urban population is divided very unevenly. More than 60% reside within the six prefectures of Tokyo, Kanagawa (Yokohama), Aichi (Nagoya), Osaka, Kyoto and Hyogo (Kobe); one-third live in Tokyo or Osaka. Although the Tokyo prefecture is almost entirely urban, there are prefectures in Tohoku, Shikoku and Kyushu that are less than 25% urban.

The distribution of the population is the result of both birth rates specific to each region and migration from one region to another. While rural, less populated areas tend to have higher birth rates, this natural advantage is offset by the constant migration from them to industrially advanced regions. Further, most of the migrants, both men and women, are in their prime reproductive years, while those who remain in rural zones are much older. All large metropolises except Tokyo (where the cost of living is prohibitively high) record more arrivals than departures. As in other postindustrial societies, the urban shift appears to have peaked and in fact declined to 1.8% in 1980–85, compared to 15% in 1960–65, when migration accounted for some 86% of overall urban growth. Whereas formerly university students remained in urban areas after completing their studies, increasing numbers of them are returning to their birthplaces in regional towns and villages, a phenomenon known as "J-turn" or "U-turn."

After peaking in 1971, Japan's marriage rate fell steadily, to an all-time low of 6.1 marriages per 1,000 in 1985. The average age for first marriage rose during the same period, from 26.8 for men and 24.2 for women to 28.2 for men and 25.5 for women. The percentage of unmarried women in the 20–35 age group also has risen rather steeply. A parallel phenomenon is the sharp rise in divorce rates, which peaked at 1.51 per 1,000 in 1983; they declined to 1.39 in 1985. However, a substantial percentage of divorces are among middle-aged and elderly couples who have lived together for 10 or more years.

The average household consists of 3.22 persons. The rapid nuclearization of families that occurred during the period of high industrialization in the 1960s has continued, although at a slower place, and nuclear families (couples living alone or with children) now account for 61% of all households. The number of households consisting of only elderly persons has increased correspondingly. More than one-third of households consisting of couples living alone includes at least one member aged 65 or over. The number of single elderly people has jumped 85% in the past decade and now accounts for 17% of all single-member households.

External emigration is not a significant demographic factor. In 1985, a total of 480,700 Japanese were living overseas, including 165,300 in North America, 154,500 in South America and 68,100 in Western Europe. The figures do not include second-generation Japanese in countries such as the United States and Brazil who have become fully integrated with their respective national populations.

Family planning, primarily through the use of contraceptives, is universally accepted and supplemented by abortion, which is legally available on a fee-for-service basis. Unlike in Western societies, abortion does not have any moral implications for the Japanese, and an anti-abortion lobby is virtually nonexistent.

DEMOGRAPHIC INDICATORS 1986

Population: 122,626,038 (1988)
Year of last census: 1985
 Sex ratio: Male 49.2 Female 50.8
Population trends (million)
 1930: 64,450   1960: 93,419   1990: 124,275
 1940: 73,075   1970: 103,720   2000: 132,589
 1950: 83,200   1980: 116,807
Population doubling time in years at current rate: over
   100
Hypothetical size of stationary population (million): 119
Assumed year of reaching net reproduction rate of 1:
   2030
Age profile (%)
 0–14: 20.4   30–44: 23.2   60–74: 8.5
 15–29: 21.0   45–59: 19.7   Over 75: 7.2
Median age (years): 37.1
Density   per sq. km. (per sq. mi.): 323.2 (837.0)
Annual growth rate (%)
 1950–55: 1.43   1975–80: 0.91   1995–2000: 0.40
 1960–65: 0.99   1980–85: 0.57   2000–2005: 0.29
 1965–70: 1.07   1985–90: 0.43   2010–2015: –0.09
 1970–75: 1.33   1990–95: 0.40   2020–2025: –0.15
Vital statistics
 Crude birth rate, 1/1000: 11.4
 Crude death rate, 1/1000: 6.2
 Change in birth rate, 1965-84: –32.6%
 Change in death rate, 1965-84: –2.8%
 Dependency, (total): 42.4
 Infant mortality rate, 1/1000: 5.3
 Child (0–4 years) mortality rate, 1/1000: (.) insignifi-
   cant
 Maternal mortality rate, 1/100,000: 15.3
 Natural increase, 1/1000: 5.2
 Total fertility rate: 1.8
 General fertility rate: 45
 Gross reproduction rate: 0.83
 Marriage rate, 1/1000: 6.1
 Divorce rate, 1/1000: 1.4
 Life expectancy, males (years): 75.1
 Life expectancy, females (years): 80.8
 Average household size: 5.4
 % illegitimate births: 0.8
Youth
 Youth population 15–24 (000): 18,808
 Youth population in 2000 (000): 15,890
Women
 Of childbearing age 15–49 (000): 31,436
 Child: Woman ratio 237
Urban
 Urban population (000): 94,588

```
DEMOGRAPHIC INDICATORS 1986 (continued)
% Urban 1965: 67 1985: 76
Annual urban growth rate (%)
   1965-80: 2.1 1980-85: 1.8
% urban population in largest city: 22
% urban population in cities over 500,000: 42
Number of cities over 500,000: 9
Annual rural growth rate: –0.1%
```

ETHNIC COMPOSITION

Ethnic Japanese constitute the vast majority of the population, as they have for well over 1,000 years.

According to tradition, the Japanese people reached the archipelago from the south, possibly through the Ryukyus. More likely, some of the original groups came from coastal regions of China and others from Siberia via the Strait of Korea, commingling on the islands to form the present-day stock. When they arrived they found the Ainu already well settled, but gradually pushed them northward—but not without some crossbreeding. Being of different racial strains, the Japanese present many different physical types. Some are slim and fair-skinned with a straight or slightly hooked nose and delicate joints. Others are rather short and stocky, dark-skinned, and with a small, sometimes flattened nose. However, they differ from other Mongoloids in their short legs.

Three principal minority groups can be identified: the *burakumin*, the Ainu and the Koreans. Although ethnically and culturally Japanese and physically indistinguishable from them, the *burakumin* are an outcast group and heavily discriminated against in public life. Their status stems from their historical association with trades involving blood and death, such as butchering, or menial work, such as tanning and shoemaking. Liberation movements and government policy have not entirely erased this stigma.

Although Koreans have lived in Japan for many centuries, they are treated as inferiors and listed as resident aliens in the census. Some are more recent arrivals, having been brought as laborers when Korea was a Japanese colony. Numbering 683,300 in 1985, they also are subject to discrimination in education, marriage and employment.

The pure Ainu number only about 16,000, and their position is similar to that of the American Indians in the United States. They are confined to a small area of the island of Hokkaido, where their ancestors took refuge from the Japanese invaders. The Ainu belong to a proto-Caucasoid, non-Mongoloid group, but some of their physical features have baffled anthropologists, who have not been able to classify them precisely. They have relatively hirsute features, uncommon among Asians. There is a strong movement among the younger Ainu to restore their cultural heritage, lost through Japanese hegemony.

These three minorities apart, Japan is one of the most ethnically homogeneous nations in the world. Indeed, homogeneity is one of its prime social strengths. Its members are unified not only by a common language, history and culture, but also by a common body of concepts about social order. An equally prominent characteristic, and one that flows from the great value placed on shared ethnicity, is the dislike of anything exotic or foreign. Outsiders are invariably considered as "polluters," and discrimination against them is acceptable and even legitimate. The number of foreigners resident in Japan has historically been insignificant. In 1985, a total of 167,300 foreigners were registered at the census, the largest group being 29,000 Americans.

LANGUAGES

The official and the sole national language is Japanese. Most linguists consider that Japanese is in a language class by itself, although there is some inconclusive evidence that places it within the Malayo-Polynesian language family. Written Japanese originally used only adapted Chinese characters (kanji), to which phonetic characters (kana) were added in the 8th century. Since 1945 both types have been simplified, their number reduced and romanized writing introduced.

English is taught as a second language in schools, and most educated Japanese have a working knowledge of English.

RELIGIONS

Japanese society has been described as highly secularistic, and indifference and skepticism in regard to religious beliefs are widespread. Such secularism reflects the profound impact of Confucian ethical concepts, which deal more with moral prescriptions about right social conduct than with the supernatural. The approach to religion is eclectic and tolerant. No conflict is felt in simultaneously holding to beliefs drawn from Shintoism and Buddhism—the predominant religions—or even Christianity, as long as they are selected and modified to suit the temperament of the people and their social needs. Despite such secularism, religious observances are conspicuous as communal and social acts valuable in themselves without any religious underpinnings. Religion is not a major issue in national life, and there are few religious leaders who exert an influence beyond their own denominational bailiwicks. Like society, politics has tended to impose its values on religion rather than vice versa.

Shintoism is the ancestral religion of the nation. It came under the influence of Confucianism in the fifth century, then was eclipsed by Buddhism from the seventh to the ninth centuries before its revival during the Meiji Era. Having lost its dogmatic role, it became a national cult to which all citizens had to submit. The supression of the state Shintoism in 1945 and the emperor's declaration that he was no longer divine swept away the state-based Shintoism, but on the other hand gave rise to a large number of heterogeneous sects of Shinto inspiration. Most of these sects are now incorporated within the Association of Shinto Shrines (Jinja-honcho). As a rule Shintoism includes all groups that revere the Japanese gods *(kami)*. Shintoism is a collective more than an individual religion, although more recently some Shinto groups have begun to emphasize spiritual and to deemphasize local and familial concerns. Shinto sects have two universities, one in Tokyo and the other in Ise.

Buddhism was introduced into Japan in the sixth century and has been the country's principal religion since the seventh century. Its evolution has been marked by the rise and spread of over 13 sects *(shu)* and 56 denominations, of which the most popular are the Tendai, Shingon, Jodo, Nichiren, Zem, Soto, Obaku and Nara. The once-flourishing Tendai school, a fountainhead of Buddhist philosophical thought, once completely dominated Japanese Buddhism. Its temples on Mount Hiei, near Kyoto, known collectively as the Enryakuji, shelter thousands of priests who practice very rigorous asceticism. The Shingon also is monastically oriented but has a much larger following who find its doctrines based on Tantric Buddhism—including mystical gestures and incantations of magical formulas—more practical for worldly gain. Shingon teaches that communion with Dai Nichi, the cosmic Buddha, can be achieved through placating and invoking lesser deities. Its center at Koya-San consists of a small city with a university and one of the finest libraries in the world. The Rinzai, Soto and Obaku sects of Zen Buddhism arrived from China in the 12th, 13th and 17th centuries, respectively, and represent a further development of the Ch'an School of meditation. All have had a profound influence on Japanese culture, including the arts, gardens, the tea ceremony, etc. Zen's continued expansion both in Japan and in the Western world is connected in part to its long association with the samurai and its techniques of discipline and austerity, particularly zazen and sanzen.

The fastest-growing Buddhist sects are its two pietist schools: Amida Jodo (Pure Land) and Nichiren. Jodo-shu and its reform wing, Jodoshin-shu, have the largest number of followers of any sect. From its major temple, Nishi Honganji, Jodoshin-shu has expanded worldwide, promoting the cult of Amida Buddha. Founded in the 13th century by the monk Nichiren, the school of Buddhism that bears his name is characterized by fanatic ardor and nationalism. Among its offshoots are the Soka Gokkai and its former political wing, the

Komeito. The Nara sects are of little importance other than the historical importance of their temples.

The term "New Religions" covers a variety of groups founded in this century (as well as some in the 19th century) in response to 20th-century problems. Many of them are not discrete religions, but only renewals or new religious movements or sects within Shintoism or Buddhism, some more radical and innovative than others. The first of the New Religions (called Shinko Shukyo in Japanese) were formed in the 19th century at the beginning of the Meiji Restoration: Tenrikyo in 1838 and Konkokyo in 1859. The New Religions have had three periods of marked development: the first in about 1920, the second in about 1938 and the third during the 1945–55 decade, corresponding, respectively, to the three periods of most rapid social change: after World War I, after the Sino-Japanese War and after the defeat in World War II. They share some common beliefs: promise of salvation, miracles and the practice of magic, shamanism, authoritarianism, syncretism and community morale. A total of 86 of the new religions belong to the Union of New Religious Organizations, including all the major ones excluding Soka Gokkai, Reiyukai, Seicho no Ie (House of Growth) and Sekai Kyusei-kyo (Church of World Messianity).

Christianity is the religion of a tiny minority and is viewed with disfavor by the majority of the Japanese as a Western institution. It was not until the Townsend Harris Treaty of 1858 that Protestants were allowed entry, and even then they were initially confined to Yokohama and Nagasaki. The first Protestant baptism did not take place until 1864. In 1878 all anti-Christian restrictions were removed. Work spread to Osaka, Kobe, Kyoto and even as far north as Hokkaido. Then a reaction against Christianity set in, and the 1890 *Imperial Rescript on Education* rejected Christian morality and theology and ordered all Japanese to revere the ancestral Shinto gods publicly. During the 15-year period from the overthrow of the Meiji Restoration regime in 1912, Christianity again gained ground, but by the 1930s the government began to insist on universal subservience to Shintoism as an act of political loyalty to the emperor and his plans for the conquest of Asia. In 1940, in order to gain full control, the government ordered the formation of the Kyodan, bringing all Protestant churches in a single United Church of Christ. Denominations that refused to join ceased to exist officially. Following the war General of the Army Douglas MacArthur called for 1,000 missionaries from the United States to resume the work of evangelization of Japan. The call was answered by over 2,500.

The first Catholic missionary to Japan was St. Francis Xavier, who founded the first mission, in Kogoshima, in 1549. Catholicism expanded rapidly, and there were 300,000 Catholics baptized by 1593, many in the Nagasaki region. However, the authorities banned Christianity in 1613, and severe persecution followed. Foreign missionaries were not able to return until 1858. The Catholic Church is divided into 16 archdioceses, of which that of Nagasaki has the greatest concentration of believers. A large number of Catholics in Nagasaki are the descendants of the Old Christians (Kirishitan) who survived the 245-year persecution. Rediscovered by Christians in 1865, all but 33,000 of these rejoined the church. Those who did not join are known as Hidden Christians (Kakure Kirishitan) or Separated Christians (Hanare). Their ceremonies and rites include Buddhist and Shinto elements. There are smaller indigenous churches formed by Japanese nationals in protest against foreign missionary domination.

HISTORICAL BACKGROUND

Recent archaeological finds show evidence of human settlements in Japan as early as 50,000 B.C. After the Paleolithic period, ending in about 11,000 B.C., three cultural eras have been identified: The Jomon (Rope-Pattern), from 11,000 to 300 B.C., was followed by the Yayoi, lasting roughly to A.D. 300 and during which waves of immigrants from China and Korea introduced wet rice cultivation and the use of bronze and iron implements. The tomb culture lasted from 300 to 600. It was not until about the fifth century that Japan emerged from its prehistoric past. By that time a centralized, clan-based authority had been firmly established in the fertile Yamato Plain in west-central Honshu. The most powerful of these clans was the Yamato, whose authority extended to Korea, called Mimana (Kaya or Karak in Korean). The supremacy of the clan was ensured in part by nurturing the myth of the clan's divine descent from the Sun Goddess through the first emperor, Jimmu, progenitor of the house that reigns today. During the formative centuries through the eighth, China, known under the name of Wo (Dwarf), was the principal source of cultural borrowing. In the fifth century Confucian texts and Chinese characters were brought to Japan by Korean scholars. Buddhism came in the next century, again through Korea, and with imperial blessing became the vehicle for the transmission of Chinese civilization to Japan. In 604 the Chinese calendar also was adopted. During the Sui and Tang dynasties in China, Japan sent regular embassies to China.

Between 645 and 702 a centralized bureaucracy was organized on the model of China, and in 710 a permanent national capital was set up at Nara. The country was divided into provinces and districts headed by governors appointed by the emperor. In practice, the authority of the central government was nominal, as real power has fallen into the hands of the Fujiwara clan, who had become dominant through intermarriage with the Yamato family. The first conscripted army of foot soldiers was created, although it proved ineffective against the Ainu. During the Nara era, Buddhism became entrenched as the faith of the court and the aristocracy and posed a growing threat to the secular authority. In 784 the capital was moved to Nagaoka and then to Heian, or modern Kyoto, where it remained until 1868.

The Heian (Kyoto) period from 794 to 1185 is celebrated for the flowering of Japanese classical culture. The introduction of the indigenous phonetic sylla- bary known as *kana* made possible the production of literary works, the great- est of which was the *Genji Monogatari* (Tales of Genji), written in about 1100 by Lady Shikibu Murasaki. Politically the Fujiwara wielded such immense power that the three centuries to 1160 sometimes are called the Fujiwara period.

After the 10th century, Fujiwara power began to wane as the wealthier local strongmen (the forerunners of the samurai) organized private governments. Progressively the rivalry among these local military clans intensified. By the 12th century two great clans, Genji and Heike, emerged out of this chaos. An epic struggle between these two clans ended in Genji victory in 1185, ushering in what is known as the feudal period. This 700-year period of rule by military overlords began formally in 1192, when Minamoto Yoritomo, who had estab- lished his *bakufu* (military government) at Kamakura, near modern Tokyo, as- sumed the title of shogun, relegating the emperor to the role of a *roi faineant*. The shogun appointed the provincial military governors (known as *daimyos*) and stewards in public and private landed estates with the right to collect taxes. The military, or samurai, class that crystallized during this period comprised lords, mounted armored noblemen and foot soldiers. It became the ruling class responsible for both civil and military functions while maintaining the fiction of imperial rule.

From the death of Yoritomo to 1568 the country was torn by constant civil strife. In the 13th century, when the Hojo clan had seized the reins of power, the country suffered two Mongol invasions, in 1274 and 1281. From the second Japan was saved only by a typhoon, which wrecked the invaders' fleet. The Kamakura shogunate ended in 1333 and was followed by the Ashikaga shogu- nate of Ashikaga Takauji, whose power base was the *bakufu* of Muromachi near Kyoto; hence the period from 1338 to 1573 is also known as the Muroma- chi period. The authority of the shogunate deteriorated after the War of Im- perial Succession (1467–77), during which the imperial and Ashikaga families split into warring camps. Kyoto and its vicinity were laid waste during the con- flict. As the shogunate became debilitated, the *daimyos* moved into the power vacuum. By the middle of the 16th century over two-thirds of the country had fallen into the hands of some 200 *daimyos*, who wielded absolute civil and mili- tary authority within their fiefs. Many of the new *daimyos* were of nonaristo- cratic samurai origins but seized power through their military prowess. Peasant revolts, often led by impoverished samurai, were common.

Reunification was finally achieved by a military triumvirate—Oda Nobunaga (1534–82), Toyotomi Hideyoshi (1536–98) and Tokugawa Ieyasu (1542–1616). The first *daimyo* to make effective use of muskets, Nobunaga gained control in 1568 and abolished the shogunate in 1573. He demolished the most powerful of the great Buddhist monasteries around Kyoto and captured the castle monastery of Osaka. His success broke the temporal power of the Buddhist sects permanently. After Nobunaga was assassinated in 1582, his vassal and ablest commander, Hideyoshi, completed the unification of the country with the title of *kampaku* (civil chancellor). Hideyoshi launched two invasions of Korea, which were cut short by his death in 1598. He was succeeded by Ieyasu, who defeated a coalition of challengers at Sekigahara in 1600. Three years later he was appointed shogun by the emperor and established his *bakufu* in Edo, today modern Tokyo. The Tokugawa period lasted for the next 250 years.

Ieyasu's first step was to consolidate his power over the *daimyos*, who were stripped of their autonomy. The samurai class was transformed into a hereditary privileged warrior-bureaucratic group prohibited from intermarrying with peasants. The political stability of the Tokugawa period was based on a rigid class structure and a policy of national seclusion. Official edicts prescribed the functions and standards of behavior of each class. Derived from both samurai and Confucian ideals, they stressed absolute loyalty to the ruler and filial piety to the family heads. Confucian ethics, with their emphases on status distinctions, paternalism and lord-vassal relationships, were well suited to the political needs of the shogunate. There was no concept of social equality. Criminal provisions applied differently to each of the four classes, and the samurai class was, for all practical purposes, exempt from any legal liability. Prolonged domestic tranquility led in the course of time to growth in internal commerce, urban centers, public works and a new merchant class. Roads were built and a rapid courier service was introduced. A money economy developed along with credit institutions. An effective centralized bureaucracy was established. A corps of inspectors, or censors, acting as secret police, informed the shogun of potential trouble spots. The Tokugawa period also was marked by the surging of new intellectual currents. Along with an interest in "national learning" and heritage spearheaded by Motoori Norinaga (1730–1801) there was an increasing interest in Western learning *(yogaku)* or Dutch learning *(ran'gaku)*, terms interchangeably applied to the study of Western science, medicine and languages. There also was a rapid expansion of Confucian-based educational facilities and a rise in literacy.

The collapse of the Tokugawa shogunate came not from within but from without, through a most unlikely incident: the arrival of U.S. warships under

Commodore Matthew C. Perry in 1853, with demands that included facilities for trade. Unable to offer resistance, the *bakufu* acquiesced. In 1854 the first of Japan's modern-day treaties was signed with the United States. The demands of the other Western powers then resulted in similar pacts with Russia, Great Britain and the Netherlands. A decade of turmoil and confusion followed over the question of opening Japan to foreigners. The antiforeign samurai coalition was inspired by Yoshida Shoin, a Choshu scholar who called for national unity under the emperor and military preparedness not only to preserve Japan's integrity but also to bring Korea, Manchuria and Taiwan under Japanese hegemony. Executed in 1859, he was to become the patron saint of Japanese ultranationalistic chauvinism. Political initiative shifted into the hands of young reformist samurai bureaucrats of Satsuma, Choshu, Tosa and Hizen, who together defeated the forces of the shogun in 1867, forcing the 15th Tokugawa shogun to lay down his office. Imperial rule was formally restored on January 3, 1868, to Emperor Matsuhito, who took the reign title of Meiji (Enlightened Rule) signaling the entry of Japan into the modern era. In 1869 the imperial capital was moved to Tokyo (Eastern Capital), ending the dual capital system that had prevailed since the 12th century.

This Meiji period lasted until 1912. As part of the new order, the Meiji government promised to open Japan to Western knowledge, and to jettison "the evil customs of the past" to bring about the unity of all classes, to give commoners freedom of choice in occupations and to establish deliberative assemblies. The process of breaking with the centuries-old feudal system was not without difficulties. Samurai dissatisfaction erupted sporadically in many local revolts and a major national one: that led by Saigo Takamori, which was crushed in 1877. The nucleus of the Meiji power structure consisted of some 100 young samurai leaders and a few court nobles. Centralization of power and modernization were set in motion under the direction of a new Council of State, which combined both legislative and executive functions. In 1869 the *daimyos* were persuaded to surrender their lands to the state; two years later the fiefs were legally abolished and reconstituted for administrative purposes into 72 prefectures and three municipalities. Another step in the relaxation of political structures was the formation of parties: the Liberal Party in 1881 and the Progressive Party in 1882. Although they failed to evoke popular support, the appearance of a rudimentary opposition persuaded the government to create a constitutional government as promised. The Meiji Constitution was promulgated in 1889 as an imperial gift to the people. Patterned after the Prussian model, the charter vested sovereignty in a divine emperor, who nevertheless remained only a figurehead. The real effect of the Constitution was to give legal sanction to the power already exercised by the bureaucracy and the military. A few civil liberties were granted but subject to abrogation by law. The bicameral legislature, the Imperial Diet, had two houses with equal powers, the House of Peers and the elective lower House of Representatives. The civil cabinet, headed by a prime minister, was responsible only to the emperor. Suffrage was limited to male property owners, who constituted 1% of the population.

On the economic front, the Meiji leaders laid the foundations of modern industry and finance. The first family conglomerates, known as *zaibatsu*, were founded during this period. The Bank of Japan was established in 1882 as the country's central bank. Not surprisingly, military modernization was given top priority by the government. By the 1880s defense expenditures accounted for one-third of the national budget annually. Under Yamagata Aritomo, the father of the Japanese Army, a German style of army organization was adopted under a general staff. In the 1880s the Meiji army had an effective strength of 73,000.

In the 1870s Japan secured sovereignty over nearby islands to the north and south: the northern portion of the Kuril Islands from Russia; the Ryukyu Islands, including Okinawa, from China, and the Bonin Islands. To enhance its stature as a world power, Japan persuaded the Western powers to cancel the unequal treaties forced on it in the mid-19th century. First Britain in 1894 and the other powers by 1899 surrendered their extraterritorial rights and relinquished tariff benefits. In 1894 Japan went to war with China over Korea. The 1895 Treaty of Shimonoseki, in the wake of Japan's quick victory, ceded to Japan Taiwan, the Pescadores Islands and the Liaodong Peninsula in southern Manchuria. The treaty provoked Russia, France and Germany to intervene on behalf of China and force Japan to renounce her claims over Korea and Manchuria. In February 1904 the Japanese government launched a surprise attack on Russian positions in Port Arthur on the Liaodong Peninsula. Two days later Japan declared war and advanced from Korea into Manchuria. The Russians were defeated in major land and naval battles. The Treaty of Portsmouth in New Hampshire in 1905, under which the Japanese won their territorial objectives in Korea and Manchuria, marked the rise of Japan as a major world power in the 20th century. In 1910 Korea was annexed as an integral part of the Japanese empire. By 1912, when the Meiji Restoration closed with the death of Emperor Matsuhito, Japan was the dominant power in East Asia.

The period from 1912 to 1926 is known as the Taisho period. The power base was broadened as the result of the extension of popular suffrage and the rise of pluralistic interest groups and political parties. The power structure became coalitional inasmuch as no single pressure or regional group could predominate, as the Satsuma-Choshu faction had done during the Meiji Restoration. Party rule began in 1918, when the first cabinet was formed based on parliamentary majority. Japan was one of the Big Five powers at the Versailles Peace Conference and in 1922 was recognized as the world's third-leading naval power at the Washington Naval Conference.

By 1926, when the Showa reign began with the accession of Emperor Hirohito, Japanese foreign policy making had fallen under the control of right-wing fascists whose goal was to make China a Japanese satellite. They were imbued with a firm belief in the divine mission of the Japanese people to conquer Asia, as well as their racial superiority over others. Most influential in the rise of military influence was the Japanese army stationed in Manchuria known as the Kwantung Army. Ultranationalism, however, was not confined to the barracks. The Black Dragon Society (a name derived from the Chinese name for the Amur River in northeastern Manchuria), whose objective was the expansion of Japan's borders to the Amur River, included thousands of civilians as well as soldiers. The Mukden incident of 1931, involving an explosion on the Manchurian rail lines, started a series of events that culminated in army control of political power in Japan. Alleging Chinese sabotage, the Kwantung Army occupied all of Manchuria by 1932, presenting the Tokyo government with a fait accompli. In February 1932 Manchuria was transformed into the puppet state of Manchukuo. The Manchurian coup was followed by a series of assassinations of moderate political leaders by ultranationalists. The last party-controlled government ended with the assassination of Prime Minister Takashi Inukai in May 1932. Thereafter Japan was under the effective rule of a fascist army. When confronted by opposition from Western powers to its expansionism, Japan began to move closer to the Axis Powers and in 1936 joined Germany and Italy in a pact against the Soviet Union. The second half of the 1930s saw remarkable economic progress in which rearmament played an important role.

For the Japanese military high command, China now became an obsession. War with China broke out in July 1937 as a minor clash near Beijing provided a further pretext for greater Japanese involvement. Shanghai and Nanjing fell to the Japanese by the end of 1937. The Chinese government moved its capital from Nanjing to Hangzhou and from there to Chongqing in 1938. With the Japanese capture of Canton in 1938 most of China's Pacific seaboard was in enemy hands.

Early German successes in World War II encouraged the Japanese government of General Hideki Tojo to conclude the Tripartite Alliance with Nazi Germany and Italy and to launch an all-out attack against Western powers in the Pacific region. Pearl Harbor was attacked on December 7, 1941, virtually crippling the U.S. Navy. Attacks west of the international date line followed on December 8. Mutual declarations of war followed. Impressive initial victories led to the conquest of all of the Far East and South Asia in a few months. By mid-1942 Japan was on the doorstep of India and poised for a sweep of the Pacific.

The tide of war turned in January 1943 with the loss of Guadalcanal. With the loss of Saipan in 1944, Japan was on the defensive. The Philippines were reconquered in the winter of 1944-45. In 1945 the Potsdam Declaration called for the unconditional surrender of Japan and its occupation by Allied forces. As Japan waited to make its decision, the world's first atomic bombs in warfare were dropped on Hiroshima and Nagasaki on August 6 and August 9, 1945, respectively. On August 8 the Soviet Union declared war against Japan. On August 14 Japan accepted the terms of the Postdam Declaration. Formal surrender was signed aboard the U.S.S. *Missouri* on November 2. General of the Army Douglas MacArthur took office as the supreme commander of the Allied forces occupying Japan.

The cost of defeat was enormous. Japan lost Korea, Taiwan, Manchuria, the Ryukyus, the Bonins, southern Sakhalin, the Kurils and the Micronesian territories in the Pacific. A total of 30% of the Japanese were homeless. Over 2.3 million soldiers were killed or wounded, and there were over 800,000 civilian casualties. Most major cities except Kyoto were heavily damaged. The economy was in ruins. The yen was worth barely a fraction of its prewar value. More than 6.5 million soldiers and civilians had to be repatriated from the Asian continent and the Pacific, sharply increasing the demand for food and services.

CONSTITUTION & GOVERNMENT

The institutional foundation of Japanese political and governmental system is the MacArthur Constitution of 1947, which replaced the 1889 Meiji Constitution (Teikoku Kempo). The ideological bases of the new Constitution were popular sovereignty, human rights and the renunciation of war. It made a clean break with the basic principles of the Meiji Constitution. Nowhere is this more evident than in the preamble, which states that "sovereign power resides with the people," a concept totally alien to Japanese history. Whereas the Meiji Constitution was described as a gift of the emperor to his subjects, the 1947 Constitution is bestowed by the people on themselves. Some of its principles of natural rights are essentially Western and conflict with the Meiji concepts of the uniqueness of the Japanese polity *(kokutai)* and the emperor's divine rights.

The role of the emperor in the political system was drastically redefined. On January 1, 1946, at the prompting of MacArthur, Emperor Hirohito made a speech renouncing his status as a divine ruler, although remaining as chief of state. In the first article of the Constitution he is described as being "the symbol of the state and of the unity of the people, deriving his position from the will of the people, with whom resides sovereign power." The emperor's powers under the old Constitution were broad and undefined. His functions under the new one are narrow, specific and largely ceremonial. Under Article 4, he has no powers relating to government. The real significance of the change in the emperor's status is that it precludes a bureaucratic or military clique from exercising broad powers in "the emperor's name." The "highest organ of state power" is the National Diet, and it is accountable to the people, not to the monarch.

A prominent feature of the Constitution is its careful and comprehensive enumeration of the "rights and duties of the people." It reaffirms the rights granted by the Meiji Constitution, including the right to serve in public office; the right to a trial according to law; and the rights to private property, freedom of movement and choice of residence; removes restrictions on certain other freedoms under the old constitutions, such as freedom of religion, freedom of speech and freedom of association; and grants new ones, including a number of new welfare rights, such as the rights to minimum standards of wholesome and cultured living, the right to equal education, the right to work and the right to unionize. Church and state are separated, and every citizen is guaranteed freedom of thought and conscience. Equality of the sexes and the right of marriage on mutual consent are recognized.

Perhaps the most striking and controversial feature of the Constitution is Article 9, renouncing war, thus essentially linking democracy with pacifism. Article 9 has two paragraphs. The first states that the Japanese people "forever renounce war as a sovereign right of the nation" and reject "the threat or use of force as a means of settling international disputes." The second paragraph states that "land, sea and air forces, as well as other war potential, will never be maintained."

Along with the divestment of imperial authority, the Constitution also abolished many props of imperial rule that had served as bastions of privilege. Powerful court offices such as lord keeper of the privy seal and grand chamberlain were abolished, along with the imperial household ministry. In their place a much more modest imperial household agency was established to administer the affairs of the imperial family. The peerage and all titles of nobility were abolished with the exception of the immediate imperial family. In addition, all other institutional power bases of the nobility were abolished, including the councils of elder statesmen (genro) and senior statesmen (jushin), whose role had been to select the prime minister, the Privy Council and the House of Peers.

Controversy over the origins of the Constitution has been a constant, if muted, theme in postwar Japanese politics. Most observers agree that it would not have been written without pressure from MacArthur, and many claim that it is a completely American document that the Japanese were forced to accept at the time. The awkwardness of the wording in Japanese lends support to the view that it was originally composed in English. Whatever its origin, it has proved a workable document, and it has never been seriously challenged. Initially it found wide acceptance, whether from a genuine desire for change or simply from the unique Japanese capacity to "accept the unacceptable." However, the Constitution was an idea whose time had come, and its philosophical bases have been reinforced by postwar social trends. Its relevance is attested to by the determined resistance of opposition parties to any movement by conservatives to revise it to make it more authentic. This resistance has been successful largely because the document is extremely difficult to amend. Amendments to the Constitution require a minimum two-thirds vote in the two houses of the Diet before they can be presented to the people in a referendum. Further, even the conservative Liberal Democratic Party has been able to fashion a policy-making process congenial to their interests within the framework of the Constitution.

The cabinet system was adopted in Japan in 1885 and has continued without interruption until the present. Despite the apparent continuity, there have been a number of fundamental changes in the powers, functions and composition of the cabinet. The postwar cabinet is based on the British model—i.e., the Constitution vests supreme executive authority in the cabinet, with the cabinet being responsible to the legislature. The prewar cabinet system was based on the Prussian model—the cabinet was not responsible to the legislature, and the legislature had no power either to select a prime minister or to dissolve the cabinet. In addition, prewar cabinets shared executive power with a number of other more or less coequal offices and institutions. The ambiguous role of the cabinets before 1947 is indicated by the fact that a cabinet was not specifically provided for in the Meiji Constitution.

The MacArthur Constitution introduced two major kinds of changes in the cabinet system. First, executive power was vested solely in the prime minister and his cabinet. Most of the cabinet's prewar competitors, such as the *genro* and *jushin* councils, the Privy Council and the Supreme Council, disappeared after 1947. To remove any ambiguities in the exercise of authority, the cabinet and all other executive institutions are placed under the control of the prime minister, as head of government. The prime minister, no longer simply the first among equals, now enjoys the power both to appoint and to remove all cabinet members at will. To hold the military in check, the National Defense Agency has been denied ministerial status and has been made subordinate to the prime minister's office. As a further guarantee against military resurgence, the Constitution requires that all cabinet members be civilians and that a majority of them be Diet members. In practice, only a small minority have come from outside the legislature. Some ministers may assume more than one portfolio because the cabinet can contain no more than 20 ministers, excluding the prime minister.

The prime minister has the authority to control and supervise all the various administrative branches of government. In addition, he is empowered to submit bills and reports on national affairs and foreign relations to the Diet, prepare the budget, administer the civil service, conduct affairs of state and conclude foreign treaties. The prime minister and the cabinet also have important judicial and legislative powers. In the judicial area, they select the chief justice and the other judges of the Supreme Court and appoint judges of the inferior courts from a list nominated by the Supreme Court. The cabinet grants pardons and amnesties. In the legislative area, the cabinet prepares and submits bills to the Diet and enacts cabinet orders to execute Diet laws.

The second major change introduced by the postwar Constitution was to establish clearly cabinet responsibility to the Diet. First, the prime minister is elected by the Diet, and in the election process the lower house plays a dominant role. The Diet can command the prime minister and the cabinet members to attend sessions of both houses, and their committees to reply to questions. Either house may adopt a resolution of impeachment against any individual cabinet member. Finally, if the lower house passes a no-confidence motion, rejects a confidence motion or fails to support a major cabinet bill, the cabinet must either resign en masse within 10 days or dissolve the lower house, call an election, and resign following the opening of the new Diet.

Postwar governments have been characterized by the growing power of the prime minister. The office has been held by a number of skilled politicians, who have held a commanding position within the ruling Liberal Democratic Party. Further, the rapid growth of the administrative state has centered on the prime minister's office *(sori fu)*, which has come to handle myriad important tasks not assigned to specific ministries. In addition to the *sori fu* proper, which maintains two offices in Chiyoda-ku, near the Diet building, there is a whole complex of offices, agencies and auxiliary organs, such as the Science Council, the Fair Trade Commission, the Administrative Management Agency, the Autonomy Agency, the Economic Planning Agency, the Defense Agency and the National Public Safety Commission. Because of the concentration of enormous power, the prime ministership has become a focus for intense political pressure.

The cabinet functions as an organic unity. Under the National Government Organization Law of 1948, all government components must maintain liaison under cabinet direction. Since Meiji times, regular cabinet meetings *(teirei kakugi)* are held every Tuesday and Friday morning, but special meetings *(rinji kakugi)* also may be held. By long-established custom, decisions are made by unanimous agreement. There is no quorum, and discussions are kept secret.

The prime minister has a number of close associates, of whom one is the deputy prime minister, with a position analogous to that of a vice president. The principal liaison between the cabinet and the special-interest groups is the chief cabinet secretary, who acts as the chief of staff. The director of the cabinet Legislative Bureau is the cabinet's legal adviser, charged with preparing draft bills and dealing with the Diet. Also attached to the cabinet is the Constitution Research Council. The National Personnel Authority (Jinji-in) is a nonpolitical, extraministerial agency administratively under the cabinet. Only the Board of Audit (Kaikei Kensa-in) is singled out in the Constitution as outside the cabinet's authority.

The turnover of ministerships in Japan is very high, and since the war, cabinets have been changed or reformed on an average of once a year. Even when the same prime minister forms a new government, he finds new men for most of the seats. Often during the lifetime of a single cabinet, there are numerous changes in personnel. The first reason is that a number of factions have to be placated with cabinet posts, and nearly every politician is afflicted with what the Japanese call *daijinbyo* (minister sickness). Second, because prime ministers may appoint and dismiss cabinet members without the approval of the Diet, they make use of this authority to strengthen their own position within the party. Major reshuffles generally reflect factional changes within the ruling party.

Under the new Constitution, the lower chamber has never been able to bring about the fall of a cabinet through a resolution of no confidence. Generally, the cabinets have survived until the convocation of a new Diet. In some cases, cabinets resigned when the prime minister stepped down on account of ill health, and in other cases on account of strikes and demonstrations or tensions within the ruling coalition.

RULERS OF JAPAN

Emperors (from 1926)

December 1926 –January 1989:	Hirohito
January 1989– :	Akihito

Prime Ministers (from 1945)

October 1945–May 1946:	Kijuro Shidehara
May 1946–May 1947:	Shigeru Yoshida (Liberal Party)
May 1947–February 1948:	Tetsu Katayama (Japan Socialist Party)
February–October 1948:	Hitoshi Ashida (Democratic Party)

ORGANIZATION OF JAPANESE GOVERNMENT

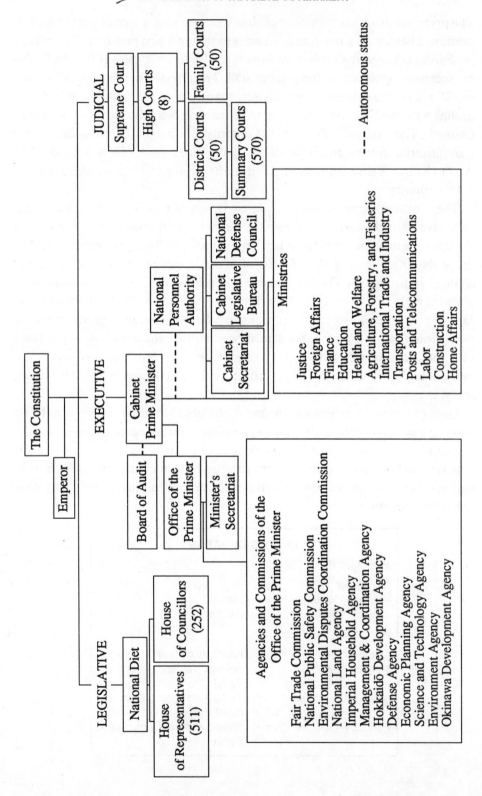

RULERS OF JAPAN *(continued)*

October 1948 –December 1954:	Shigeru Yoshida (Liberal Party)
December 1954 –December 1956:	Ichiro Hatoyama (Democratic Party, Liberal Democratic Party)
December 1956 –February 1957:	Tanzan Ishibashi (Liberal Democratic Party)
February 1957–July 1960:	Nobusuke Nishi (Liberal Democratic Party)
July 1960–November 1964:	Hayato Ikeda (Liberal Democratic Party)
November 1964–July 1972:	Eisaku Sato (Liberal Democratic Party)
July 1972–December 1974:	Kakuei Tanaka (Liberal Democratic Party)
December 1974 –December 1976:	Takeo Miki (Liberal Democratic Party)
December 1976 –November 1978:	Takeo Fukuda (Liberal Democratic Party)
November 1978 –June 1980:	Masayoshi Ohira (Liberal Democratic Party)
June–July 1980:	Masayoshi Ito (acting) (Liberal Democratic Party)
July 1980–November 1982:	Zenko Suzuki (Liberal Democratic Party)
November 1982 –November 1987:	Yasuhiro Nakasone (Liberal Democratic Party)
November 1987 –June 1989:	Noboru Takeshita (Liberal Democratic Party)
June–August 1989:	Sosuke Uno
August 1989–	Toshiki Kaifu

CABINET MEMBERS

Prime minister:	Toshiki Kaifu
Deputy prime minister	n/a
Minister of agriculture, forestry and fisheries	Michihiko Kano
Minister of construction	Shozo Harada
Minister of education	Kazuya Ishibashi
Minister of finance	Ryutaro Hashimoto

```
┌─────────────────────────────────────────────────┐
│           CABINET MEMBERS (continued)           │
│  Minister of foreign affairs      Taro Nakayama  │
│  Minister of health and welfare   Saburo Toida   │
│  Minister of home affairs         Kozo Watanabe  │
│  Minister of international trade                  │
│    and industry                   Hikaru Matsunaga│
│  Minister of justice              Masao Goto     │
│  Minister of labor                Joji Fukushima │
│  Minister of posts and telecom-                  │
│    munications                    Sempachi Oishi │
│  Minister of transportation       Takami Eto     │
│  Chief cabinet secretary          Mayumi Moriyama│
│  Director-General, Economic                      │
│    Planning Agency                Sumiko Takahara│
│  Director-General, Environment                   │
│    Agency                         Setsu Shiga    │
│  Director-General, Hokkaido De-                  │
│    velopment Agency               Fumio Abe      │
│  Director-General, Defense                       │
│    Agency                         Juro Matsumoto │
│  Director-General, Management                    │
│    and Coordination Agency        Kiyoshi Mizuno │
│  Director-General, National Land                 │
│    Agency                         Hajime Ishii   │
│  Director-General, Okinawa De-                   │
│    velopment Agency               Fumio Abe      │
│  Director-General, Science and                   │
│    Technology Agency              Eizaburo Saito │
│  Governor, Central Bank           Satoshi Sumita │
└─────────────────────────────────────────────────┘
```

FREEDOM & HUMAN RIGHTS

All civil and political rights are guaranteed by the Constitution and respected in practice. There are no restrictions on political, religious or trade union activities.

In 1987 militant Ainu groups petitioned the U.N. High Commission for Human rights against maltreatment. In the same year, mental health patients petitioned the International Commission of Jurists against alleged neglect. Groups of Okinawans also have complained in recent years of discrimination.

Resident aliens, particularly Koreans, have suffered entrenched social prejudice. Social exclusion also is practiced against the economically deprived *burakumin*, who number over 2 million. Both groups have restricted access to public housing, employment and education. In recent years the government has enacted several measures to extend to the Korean minority public benefits such as housing loans, Social Security pensions and public employment rights. Korean names are now officially pronounced according to the Korean rather than the Japanese reading of name characters. The Alien Registration Law has been revised to require only a single, one-time fingerprinting of foreign residents rather than at five intervals, as formerly. The government also has enacted the Special Measures for Regional Development Law, which provides funds until 1992 to help assimilate the _burakumin_ into the mainstream of society.

Despite the passage of the Equal Employment Opportunity Law in 1986 to prohibit discrimination on grounds of gender, women continue to suffer severe disadvantages in the marketplace. The measure has been criticized as containing no penalties for violators. Social mores discourage women from pursuing independent careers, and there are significant disparities between wage scales for males and females. According to one survey in 1987, the number of women who disagree with the statement "A woman's place is in the home" has actually decreased during the past three years.

CIVIL SERVICE

The National Public Service Law, passed in 1947 and revised in 1965, established the structure of postwar public administration. It distinguishes between special and regular categories of public servants. Appointments to the special category are governed by political and other considerations and do not involve examinations. The core of the civil service is composed of the regular category, whose members are recruited through competitive examinations. They are divided into junior service and higher professional levels.

The higher professional civil servants are an elite whose prestige in the eyes of the general public is unmatched by any other group in society. They compare themselves to the _kuroko_ (stagehands) in a Kabuki drama who set up things for the actors, while others have described them as so powerful that the government and the Diet are merely extensions of the bureaucracy. There are about 500 higher civil servants attached to each ministry, and some 10 to 20 are admitted each year after having passed through an extremely rigorous educational screening process that begins as early as middle school and culminates in the successful passage of the civil service entrance examination. The great majority are graduates of the law faculty of the University of Tokyo. As in the West, the right school ties and connections are important for career advancement. Once appointed, civil servants remain in the same ministry for the rest of their careers. Thus along with a strong legalistic attitude born of their training, the bureaucracy is characterized by a deep-rooted sense of departmentalism.

Although civil servants receive modest salaries and benefits compared to their counterparts in the private sector, and work long hours under intense pressure, they retain a strong sense of mission as guardians of the country's welfare and destiny. The ideal official is bright but not brilliant, a good team player but not an individualist. The Ministry of Finance is generally considered the most prestigious of the ministries because its Budget Bureau regulates public finance. The officials of the Ministry of Finance are described as the "samurai of the government." The Ministry of International Trade and Industry also is prestigious.

Civil servants are largely insulated from Diet pressures apart from the liability to answer questions from committee members. Civil servants also are relatively free from cabinet interference, with the exception of the few political appointees. Cabinet ministers have a short tenure, which gives them little time to initiate administrative reforms. Below the cabinet minister is the administrative vice minister, who is a career civil servant appointed in accordance with internally established principles of seniority.

A second factor in the independence of the bureaucracy from political pressures is its virtual monopoly of information. Diet members do not have a large research staff independent of the civil service. Often officials who are questioned by the Diet are also required to provide the information on which the questions are framed.

One of the most important organs of government is the interdepartmental conference of administrative and parliamentary vice ministers. Assembling twice a week, on Monday and Thursday (i.e., one day ahead of the cabinet meeting), the vice ministers are aided by the directors of the cabinet secretariat and the Legislation Bureau.

The agency primarily responsible for maintaining unified personnel standards throughout the government as well as guarding the integrity of public service is the National Personnel Authority, which consists of a president and two commissioners. Separated from the cabinet, it holds semilegislative and quasi-judicial powers. The authority is assisted by the National Personnel Council, a liaison organ for the various ministries. The authority submits annual recommendations on pay for public servants, supervises the administration of the various civil service examinations, screens candidates for appointments, provides in-service training, conducts medical tests and reviews complaints of inequity from civil servants. Perhaps its most important function is the annual revision of salary scales, which is eagerly awaited by the bureaucracy and invariably followed by protests. The authority also administers a performance rating system.

Regulations restrict the outside activities of public employees. Political involvement is considered incompatible with public service ethics. Conflict of interest also is strictly monitored, especially participation in private business during civil service employment or after leaving office.

LOCAL GOVERNMENT

Japan is divided into 43 rural prefectures *(ken)*; two urban prefectures, *(fu)*, Kyoto and Osaka; one district, Hokkaido; and one metropolitan district *(to)*, Tokyo. These jurisdictions are subdivided into cities, towns and villages. Tokyo, Osaka, Kyoto and other large cities are subdivided into wards *(ku)*, which are further split into precincts (*machi* or *cho*). All municipalities are collectively known as *shichoson.* Below them are towns, built-up villages (*mura* or *son*) and hamlets *(buraku).*

The most striking event in local government since World War II has been the amalgamation *(gappei)* of small towns and villages. The Law for the Acceleration of Amalgamation of Towns and Villages of 1953 reduced the number of towns and villages from 9,582 to a little over 3,000.

The constitutional foundations of local government are found in four articles of Chapter 8 of the Constitution. Article 92 states, "Regulations concerning the organization and operation of local public entities shall be fixed in accordance with the principle of local autonomy." Article 93 states, "The local public entities shall establish assemblies as their deliberative organs, in accordance with law. The chief executive officers of all local public entities, the members of their assemblies and such other local officials as may be determined by law shall be elected by direct popular vote within their several communities." Article 94 states, "Local public entities shall have the right to manage their property, affairs and administration and to enact their own regulations within law." Article 95, which is clearly of American origin, states, "A special law applicable only to one local public entity cannot be enacted by the Diet without the consent of the majority of the voters of the local public entity concerned, obtained in accordance with laws." Beyond these constitutional provisions, local government relies on major Diet laws, such as the Local Autonomy Law and the Local Finance Law.

Each prefecture or district has a governor and a unicameral Assembly, both elected by popular vote for a four-year term. All prefectures and districts are required by national law to maintain departments of general affairs, finance, welfare, health and labor. Departments of agriculture, fisheries, forestry, commerce and industry are optional, depending on local needs. Relationships between the governor and the Assembly are mutually restraining. The power of the Assembly to pass a vote of no-confidence against the chief prefectural executive is balanced by the governor's power to dissolve the legislature.

Cities, like prefectures and districts, are self-governing units administered independently of the larger units of which they are a part. To become a city, a town or village has to have at least 30,000 inhabitants, 60% of whom are engaged in urban occupations. It also is required to have extensive commercial facilities, and 60% of its buildings have to stand within the urban core. City government is headed by a mayor, elected by popular vote for a four-year term. A City Assembly, with varying numbers of representatives according to population, is elected at the same time. In large cities—Nagoya, Yokohama, Fukuoka, Kobe, Tokyo, Osaka and Kyoto—each ward elects an Assembly, which in turn elects ward superintendents.

POLITICAL SUBDIVISIONS

Prefectures	Capitals	Area Sq. Km.	Sq. Mi.	Population (1985 census)
Chubu				
Aichi	Nagoya	5,138	1,984	6,477,200
Fukui	Fukui	4,191	1,618	822,000
Gifu	Gifu	10,596	4,091	2,038,300
Ishikawa	Kanazawa	4,197	1,620	1,157,700
Nagano	Nagano	13,585	5,245	2,170,400
Niigata	Niigata	12,579	4,857	2,448,900
Shizuoka	Shizuoka	7,773	3,001	3,582,000
Toyama	Toyama	4,252	1,642	1,125,400
Yamanashi	Kofu	4,463	1,723	823,100
Chugoku				
Hiroshima	Hiroshima	8,466	3,269	2,820,200
Okayama	Okayama	7,090	2,737	1,914,100
Shimane	Matsue	6,628	2,559	797,500
Tottori	Tottori	3,493	1,349	620,200
Yamaguchi	Yamaguchi	6,106	2,358	1,588,500
Hokkaido				
Hokkaido (territory)	Sapporo	83,519	32,247	5,688,500
Kanto				
Chiba	Chiba	5,150	1,988	5,168,100
Gumma	Maebashi	6,356	2,454	1,913,200
Ibaraki	Mito	6,094	2,353	2,717,500
Kanagawa	Yokohoma	2,402	927	7,380,200
Saitama	Urawa	3,799	1,467	5,854,900
Tochigi	Utsunomiya	6,414	2,476	1,883,800
Kinki				
Hyogo	Kobe	8,378	3,235	5,275,600
Mie	Tsu	5,778	2,231	1,738,300
Nara	Nara	3,692	1,425	1,303,900
Shiga	Otsu	4,016	1,551	1,165,900
Wakayama	Wakayama	4,725	1,824	1,086,600
Kyushu				
Fukuoka	Fukuoka	4,960	1,915	4,753,200
Kagoshima	Kagoshima	9,165	3,539	1,833,600
Kumamoto	Kumamoto	7,408	2,860	1,836,200

POLITICAL SUBDIVISIONS *(continued)*				
Miyazaki	Miyazaki	7,735	2,986	1,183,500
Nagasaki	Nagasaki	4,112	1,588	1,599,500
Oita	Oita	6,337	2,447	1,246,300
Saga	Saga	2,433	939	890,700
Ryukyu				
Okinawa	Naha	2,254	870	1,177,000
Shikoku				
Ehime	Matsuyama	5,672	2,190	1,533,600
Kagawa	Takamatsu	1,882	727	1,034,000
Kochi	Kochi	7,107	2,744	843,400
Tokushima	Tokushima	4,145	1,600	831,400
Tohoku				
Akita	Akita	11,612	4,483	1,252,900
Aomori	Aomori	9,617	3,713	1,521,200
Fukushima	Fukushima	13,784	5,322	2,054,200
Iwate	Morioka	15,279	5,899	1,454,600
Miyagi	Sendai	7,292	2,815	2,167,900
Yamagata	Yamagata	9,327	3,601	1,251,200
Metropolis				
Tokyo	Tokyo	2,162	835	11,780,500
Urban prefectures				
Kyoto	Kyoto	4,613	1,781	2,565,400
Osaka	Osaka	1,868	721	8,653,300
TOTAL		377,801	145,870	121,025,700

The terms *machi* and *cho* designate self-governing towns outside the cities as well as the subdivisions of urban wards. Like the cities, each has its elected mayor and assembly. Such a town may be formed by the incorporation of a large village or the merger of neighboring villages. Villages are the smallest self-governing entities in the rural areas and consist of a number of hamlets *(buraku).* The principal village official is the elected mayor, who presides over a Village Council, both being elected by popular vote for a four-year term.

Under the village in the rural areas and the ward in the cities are informal units of neighborhood self-government, consisting of *chokai* or *burakukai*, subdivided into still smaller units consisting of 20 or 30 adjacent households *(han).* Although they do not have formal legal status, these informal units serve as the focus of community activity; as conduits for government programs; and as coordinators of cleanup, fire prevention, crime prevention and garbage collection activities.

Popular control over local government is exercised through the assemblies at the various levels. Their size is determined by national law and varies from 12 to 100 members, depending on the population. Assemblymen who are elected for four-year terms may be recalled by the voters, who may also demand a dissolution of the entire body. The local legislative bodies are empowered to enact bylaws *(jorei)* on subjects enumerated in the Local Autonomy Law. Only the Diet may pass laws *(horitsu)*. The governor or the mayor may veto a measure passed by the relevant Assembly, but the Assembly may pass the measure over the veto by a two-thirds vote. The Assembly may vote no confidence in the chief executive with a three-fourths majority, forcing the chief executive to resign or to dissolve the legislative body. Such no-confidence votes occur rarely. Increasingly local assemblies express their wishes to the central government in the form of resolutions, not only on local issues but on national and international issues as well.

In addition to the executive and legislative branches of local government, there are on the prefectural level, and often on the municipal level, boards of education, public safety commissions, inspection (auditing) commissions and personnel commissions made up of members usually appointed by the mayor or governor with the approval of the Assembly. These members also are subject to recall by the voters. The Local Autonomy Law provides for the exercise of initiative, recall and referendum by the voters in local entities. If one-fiftieth of the voters on the rolls sign a demand for the enactment of a bylaw, the chief executive must present the demand, together with his opinion thereon, to the local Assembly.

Under present laws, 70% of the taxes collected go to the central government and 30% to the local governments. However, the central government returns about 60% of its tax revenues to the local governments in various forms. The principal sources of local government revenues are legal and extralegal ordinary taxes; special-purpose taxes; rents and fees; and subsidies and grants. Local bodies also may raise loans with the permission of the Minister of Home Affairs or the prefectural governor. Actually, most of the loans are supplied by federal funds, since few local bodies have the financial capacity to obtain funds on the open market. Under the Local Distribution Tax Law, a percentage of certain national taxes, such as the income tax, the corporation tax and the sake tax, are distributed among local entities according to fixed formula.

Local government finances have historically suffered from inadequate resources and growing expenditures. All local taxes are prescribed by national laws, which set standard rates and exemptions. Thus local tax revenue is at the mercy of the national government from year to year. Local taxes also are so low that the local entities cannot operate without funds from the central government. Over the years the local bodies have been cast in the role of poor relations and the central government in the role of a rich but stingy uncle. To obtain disbursements from the central government, local bodies have to meet national standards. The average local body does not know the size of its operating budget until the various central government ministries decide on their subsidies and until the Home Ministry determines its share in the Local Distribution Tax. Thus the original budget of every local body is little more than a guesstimate on both the revenue and expenditure sides and undergoes constant revision depending on news from Tokyo. It is not uncommon for local entities to pass six or even more supplementary budgets in the course of a fiscal year, based on negotiations with central government agencies, even though the law does not require approval of a national agency before a local budget becomes effective.

Not only in the area of finance but also in other administrative and legislative areas, autonomy has eluded the local bodies. Few assemblies have asserted their independence vis-à-vis the local executive or the central government, even within the provisions of law. Executive-sponsored bylaws and budgets normally are passed without change. A combination of factors has influenced this subservience. One is the dominant conservatism of local politics. Traditional notions of harmony, shared by executives and legislators alike, place a taboo on the use of legal devices by which an Assembly could assert itself. But perhaps the most important factor is the narrow range of local autonomy and its lack of substance. Most local legislative activity exhausts itself in the adoption of measures handed down from above.

FOREIGN POLICY

Japan's foreign policy in the late 1980s still is undergoing a major revision that began in the early 1980s. The policy that Japan had followed throughout the postwar period was characterized by concentration on economic growth; flexible accommodation to the regional and global policies of the United States while avoiding major initiatives on its own; adherence to the pacifist principles embodied in the 1947 Constitution, also known as the "Peace Constitution"; and a generally passive and low-profile behavior in world affairs. Relations with other countries were until recently governed by what the leadership termed "omnidirectional diplomacy," essentially a policy of political neutrality in foreign affairs and expansion of economic relations. The policy was highly successful on the economic side but became unsustainable without the security umbrella provided by the United States.

A number of changes in the international political climate made Japan's old foreign policy tenets obsolete and required a rethinking of their premises. These included Japan's burgeoning economic power as the third-leading industrial nation in the world and the concomitant charges of economic aggression frequently leveled against it even by developed nations; the new détente between the United States and the Soviet Union and the United States and China and the consequent dissipation of cold war policies; the rapid reduction of U.S. military presence in Asia following the Vietnam debacle; and the oil crises of the 1970s, exposing Japan's critical vulnerability to a cutoff of raw material and energy supplies. In addition to these situational changes, a new postwar generation had risen to leadership in Japan and was clamoring for a new agenda in foreign relations that will be more positive and less dependent on the United States. The debate on foreign policy centered on some key issues: the pursuit of a more assertive diplomacy without aggravating strategic vulnerabilities; the building of a strong national security without abandoning the constitutional imperative of pacifism; the maintenance of a strong relationship with the United States in the face of strong economic pressures posed by massive balance-of-trade imbalances; and the forging of a constructive policy toward Third World relations on a political as well as an economic basis.

Japan's search for a new style in foreign relations is complicated by its historic insularity and inability to deal with international issues except in military terms (as in the first half of this century) or in purely economic terms (as in the second half). It has no ethnic or cultural allies, which so often determine the direction of bilateral relations for other countries. The predominance of economic and trade considerations and the lack of ideological ones reduce the number of options available to foreign policy makers. The memories of its World War II debacle have left scars that make Japan unwilling to adopt dramatic or radical shifts in policy that might prove costly to its present political and economic stability. Thus, even as its economic power grows, Japan may never become a political superpower, being untrained by tradition to handle such a role or to contribute other than marginally to international diplomatic debates.

The demand for a more autonomous foreign policy in Japan has hinged less on specific issues or areas than on a vague sense of national self-esteem generated by the economic miracle of the past two decades. Further, in few countries is the economic content of foreign policy so strong as in Japan. Economic security dominates foreign policy initiatives so heavily that the Ministry of International Trade and Industry (MITI) has as much influence in this field as the Ministry of Foreign Affairs. This is evident in Japan's pro-Arab tilt since the 1973 oil shock; its politically motivated aid to strategically located Third World countries; its efforts to cultivate closer relations with ASEAN; and its concern over the vital sea lanes to the Middle East.

Relations with the United States, formally embodied in the 1960 Mutual Security Treaty, remain the cornerstone of Japanese foreign policy. Despite the strains posed by economic skirmishes and an undeclared trade war between the two countries, Japanese leaders acknowledge the primacy of relations with the United States. Even as Japan has made adjustments to compensate for the lower U.S. profile in East Asia, it has been careful to avoid actions likely to damage U.S. interests in the Pacific. Although the term "alliance" is never officially used to describe U.S.-Japanese relations, it is one for all practical purposes. Under the terms of the treaty both parties assume an obligation to assist each other in case of an armed attack, but since Japan is constitutionally prohibited from sending armed forces overseas, it is a one-way provision. With the settlement of the Okinawa issue in 1972 and the return of the island to Japan, there are no major political issues between the two countries. Japan faithfully hewed the U.S. line during the cold war, and when the United States abondoned its cold war posture in the 1970s, Japan followed suit, although with some chagrin over U.S. failure to consult Japan before making such a fundamental change in foreign policy. Since the mid-1970s, economic issues have clouded relations between the two countries. They stemmed from the ever-widening U.S. trade and payments deficit with Japan, beginning in 1965, when Japan for the first time achieved an export surplus. The first issue related to Japanese exports of woolen and synthetic textiles, and it was followed by U.S. charges of dumping, restrictions on imports from the United States, and the general lack of reciprocity in trade. Relations between Washington and Tokyo were further strained by periodic monetary crises brought about by massive U.S. trade deficits. More significantly public opinion in the United States and its Western allies has turned against Japanese "economic aggression," placing Japan on the defensive. Ironically, Japan is being stigmatized as a passive military partner with a defense budget that is minuscule in terms of its national wealth, although the 1947 pacifist Constitution was a U.S. creation.

Until 1960, Japan had no political or trade relations with China. Historical antagonisms were reinforced by opposition to Chinese communism and Japan's desire not to offend the United States. Despite the Liao-Takasaki Agreement of 1962, relations remained complicated because of Japan's substantial economic ties with Taiwan and the presence of a pro-Chiang Kai-shek faction within the Liberal Democratic Party. Relations were normalized only in 1971, after China was admitted to the United Nations. In 1972 Prime Minister Kakuei Tanaka visited Beijing and signed a historic joint statement that ended nearly 80 years of enmity between the two countries. The statement recognized the Communist regime as the sole legal government of China, and Taiwan as an inalienable part of China. For its part, China waived its demand for war indemnities from Japan totaling $50 billion. A formal treaty of peace and friendship was signed in 1978, including an antihegemony clause directed primarily against the Soviet Union. Since then the thrust of Japanese policy toward China has been predominantly economic. Beijing's ambitious plans for drawing on Japanese capital and know-how for the modernization of the Chinese economy have run into technical and financial difficulties and have been scaled down a number of times. Development of the giant Baoshan steel works near Shanghai, planned as a showpiece of

Sino-Japanese cooperation, stalled in the early 1980s. There also are fears, both in China and the United States, that Japan is seeking to monopolize the Chinese market.

Even 40 years after the end of World War II, Japan and the Soviet Union do not have a peace treaty and are technically in a state of war. The main stumbling block is a territorial dispute over the islands Etorofu and Kunashiri at the southern end of the Kuril Islands chain, and the smaller Shikotan Island and Hobomai Island group northeast of Hokkaido. In the 1970s the Soviets militarized the islands, alarming the Japanese and causing a further deterioration in relations. The 1978 Sino-Japanese Treaty, with its antihegemony clause directed primiraly against the Soviet Union, was denounced by Moscow and hardened its positions against Japan. Japan was one of the few countries that responded to President Carter's call for sanctions against the Soviet Union after its invasion of Afghanistan. Other unsettled problems include Japanese fishing rights in the Sea of Okhotsk and the repatriation of Japanese prisoners of war who, the Japanese claim, still are being held in Siberian prisons. Despite these problems, Soviet-Japanese relations improved appreciably after the 1960s. Cooperation in the economic sphere expanded rapidly in the 1970s. The Soviet Union needed Japanese capital, technology and consumer goods, while Japan needed Soviet natural resources such as oil, gas, coal, iron ore and timber. By the 1980s Japan had become, next to West Germany, the Soviet Union's most important non-Communist trading partner. By the end of the decade Japan has undertaken several large-scale joint development projects with the Soviet Union despite the chill in political relations.

Japan's relations with its other Asian neighbors have moved through several transitional stages. In the face of major international changes in the regional power structure in East Asia, Japan has been forced to undertake a more active and broader role and to pursue a more positive Asian policy. Japan began normalization of relations with its neighbors in the 1950s with the payment of war reparations to Burma, Indonesia, the Philippines and South Vietnam. Japan's reintegration into the Asian scene also was facilitated by its joining the Colombo Plan in 1954 and its attendance at the Afro-Asian Conference in Bandung in 1955. With the establishment of the Overseas Economic Cooperation Fund in 1961 and the Technical Cooperation Agency in 1961, Japan entered the ranks of donors of development aid. In 1963 Japan became a full member of the OECD. Following the first Ministerial Conference on the Economic Development of Southeast Asia in 1966, Japan helped to found the Asian Development Bank under a Japanese president but with headquarters in Manila. It was harder to overcome residual fears that the Japanese aid program was a Trojan horse akin to the prewar Greater East Asia Coprosperity Sphere, and in some countries there were anti-Japanese demonstrations. In response, Prime Minister Takeo Fukuda issued the so-called Fukuda Doctrine, reaffirming Japan's antimilitarism.

With two Asian countries, relations have followed a checkered course. Japan was one of the earliest countries to recognize North Vietnam. However, when Vietnam invaded Kampuchea in 1978, Japan was embarrassed and joined ASEAN in condemning the invasion. Historically the Japanese have had little respect for the Koreans, whom they consider inferior. This ill feeling has carried over into foreign relations, and Japanese-Korean diplomacy has been marred by a number of incidents that, though minor in themselves, cumulatively hampered the development of a strong relationship. One irritant has been Japan's evenhandedness toward the two Koreas. Nevertheless, South Korea is, after the United States, Japan's largest trading partner, and there are periodic ministerial-level meetings between the two countries.

Because Japan has a clear definition of its self-interests, its conduct of foreign policy is not complicated. Since the 1970s there has been less opposition in the Diet to major elements of the policy, and house debates in this area are less lively than formerly. Under the Constitution, the prime minister is required to make periodic reports to the Diet on the state of Japanese foreign relations. Traditionally the prime ministers have taken a dominant role in foreign affairs, particularly in the conduct of personal diplomacy and the formulation of policy guidelines and responses to events and issues. The Ministry of Foreign Affairs is staffed by an elite career foreign service corps, and nearly all ambassadors are veteran diplomats rather than political appointees.

PARLIAMENT

The Japanese Diet (Kokkai) is the oldest legislature in the non-Western world. It is a bicameral legislature with a lower house called the House of Representatives (Shugiin) and an upper house called the House of Councillors (Sangiin).

The lower chamber presently consists of 512 members elected from 130 constituencies every four years. The number of members elected per constituency varies from one to five. The upper chamber, which replaced the prewar House of Peers, consists of 252 members serving six-year terms. It is renewed by halves every three years, 100 members being elected from the nation at large and the balance from prefectural units.

The structure and purpose of the Diet are defined in the Constitution, the Diet Law of 1947 and the rules of each house. Article 41 of the Constitution defines it as the "highest organ of state power." The responsibilities of the Diet include making laws, approving the national budget, drafting amendments to the

Constitution, investigating government policies and programs, electing the prime minister, impeaching judges and questioning cabinet officials.

Sessions of the Diet are of three kinds: The ordinary *(tsujo)* session is convoked in late December. A recess covering the traditional New Year's festivities ordinarily lasts until late January, whereupon the Diet is convened again for the constitutional minimum of 150 days. An extraordinary *(rinji)* session is convoked when one-fourth of all members of either house petition the cabinet. A special *(tokubetsu)* session is mandatory within 30 days of a national election or 70 days of the dissolution of old House of Representatives. The House of Representatives itself meets in a chamber that resembles more its U.S. rather than its British counterpart. Members sit in a semicircle, with members of the cabinet on one side on a raised platform. The House of Representatives meets at 1:00 P.M. after committee meetings in the morning. The House of Councillors reverses this schedule, holding its plenary session at 10:00 A.M. and committee meetings in the afternoon. Attendance generally is poor. Deliberations on the floor are public except when two-thirds of the members present vote for a secret session. Voting is done by standing, showing of hands or ballots. All decisions are by simple majority. As critical maneuvers have come to be concentrated in party caucuses and committee meetings, provisions for plenary debate, incorporated in rules for the postwar Diet, have been abandoned.

One of the most important sections of the postwar Diet Law has been the establishment of standing committees. The Standing Committee on House Management, usually referred to as the Giun, regulates the internal affairs of each chamber. The chairman of the Giun ranks just below the presiding officers of each house. Committee directors come from the ranks of each party's Diet Strategy Committee, on which all factions are represented. Thus the committee becomes a critical arena where warring or otherwise hostile camps search for areas of agreement and compromise. In the case of noncontroversial legislation the system works smoothly and the plenary session becomes nothing more than a staged formality. However, in the case of controversial issues, the system often breaks down. Discussions may become interminable, and if the Giun's members cannot arrive at a consensus, the matter is referred to a meeting of the secretaries-general of all parliamentary parties. If even they cannot find a formula that satisfies all parties, the speaker may intervene and convene a meeting of the supreme party leaders, including the prime minister. Negotiations and consultations *(hanashiai)* usually are behind the scenes and often are conducted outside the Diet in a *machiai* (literally, house of assignation). If even these negotiations do not lead to an agreement, the speaker or the president of the House of Councillors has the authority to convene a plenary session of the whole house where the majority rams the legislation through.

There are 16 standing committees, identical in name, for each house: (1) Cabinet, (2) Local Administration, (3) Judicial Affairs, (4) Foreign Affairs, (5) Finance, (6) Education, (7) Social and Labor Affairs, (8) Agriculture, (9) Commerce and Industry, (10) Transportation, (11) Postal Services, (12) Construction, (13) Budget, (14) Audit, (15) Discipline and (16) Steering. The Finance Committee is perhaps the most powerful, for it assigns, in the first instance, party strengths in the other committees. In the Budget Committee the bitterest battles are fought between the government and the opposition.

According to the Diet Law, each member must serve on at least one and on not more than three standing committees. Selection of chairman is strictly in accordance with party strengths, and thus all are headed by Liberal Democratic Party members. Training and experience rather than seniority determine membership. Committees maintain an absolute control over the flow of all bills. Although meetings are technically public, strategy is worked out behind closed doors.

The Committee on the Cabinet has broad jurisdiction. It concerns itself not only with the work of the cabinet and the prime minister's office but also with those agencies that have not yet attained the status of a ministry.

The Diet institution closest to question time in the British Parliament is the interpellations in the Budget Committee. It is a forum, sometimes televised, for questioning cabinet ministers on all matters of policy regardless of whether these queries are in any way related to an item in the budget. Attendance by cabinet ministers and other government officials whose presence has been called for is mandatory. It performs an extremely useful function in informing the public regarding specific aspects of government policy even though official replies are more often than not evasive, helped by the marvelous indirectness and ambiguity so characteristic of the Japanese language. Even though the influence of these interpellations on government policy is negligible, they provide an opportunity for interlocutors and their respondents to score points with the public, especially before elections.

The Diet Law also provides for the establishment of special committees. They may be created at any time but normally are established at the beginning of each session of the Diet. Their ostensible role is to examine matters that do not fall within the purview of the standing committees, but more commonly they are set up to focus the Diet's attention on a particularly pressing problem or to remove an issue from the influence of vested interests to which a standing committee may be unduly responsive. Many of the special committees virtually acquire the permanence of a standing committee, except that they must be formally re-created at the beginning of each session. In many cases the government favors special committees as devices to control the legislative agenda and shorten the timetable of deliberations.

Committee business is controlled by the *riji* (directors) of a committee who, with the chairman, regulate its composition and assignments. Committee assignment, determined by the leadership of each parliamentary party, is an important element in maintaining influence over the legislative process. For the ruling Liberal Democratic Party, balanced committee membership is deeply enmeshed in intraparty factional politics. The majority factions receive about three committee chairmanships; the smaller factions, no more than one apiece. Prime ministers have tended to use their power to choose committee chairmen to reward faithful faction loyalists or as an inducement to coalition allies. Having proper factional affiliations and the support of one's *oyabun* (boss) are not the only criteria for becoming a chairman. A certain amount of seniority—the average is five terms—is a prerequisite. Because of his subservience to party bosses, he is almost never able to carve out an independent fiefdom for himself, as is the case with his American counterpart. Although he wields considerable powers, both disciplinary and procedural, he is the agent of the governing party rather than a guardian of the committee's prerogatives.

Each of the Diet committees has a substantial staff headed by specialists drawn from the ranks of the senior bureaucrats. They provide the committee to which they are assigned with expert assistance, but they also contribute to the pervasive influence of the national bureaucracy in the work of the Diet. It has been charged that many of the committees have become as a result outposts of the respective departments. The Diet Law requires that Diet members be given salaries comparable to those of the highest civil servants, as well as travel and franking privileges. The budget of the legislature is under its own control rather than that of the Ministry of Finance.

The House of Representatives has the greater power of the two houses, in contrast to the prewar system, in which they were coequal. According to Article 59 of the Constitution, a bill approved by the representatives but turned down by the councillors returns to the lower house, where it becomes law if passed with a two-thirds majority. If the upper and lower houses have a disagreement on a national budget or approval of a treaty, and if it is not resolved by a joint committee of the two houses, then after 30 days the decision of the lower house prevails. Choice of the prime minister, when there is a conflict between the two houses, is decided in the same manner. Although designed by the framers of the Constitution as a nonpartisan body, the upper house became, even by the 1950s, a highly politicized body in which violent scenes are not uncommon.

Japan's first law of elections for members of the House of Representatives was promulgated in 1889. It provided that only males who were 25 years and older and who paid 15 yen or more a year in direct national taxes could vote. Voting citizens elected one member per district by open ballot. A law in 1900 brought in the secret ballot, and a law in 1925 introduced universal male suffrage.

The present electoral system is based on the Public Offices Election Law of 1950 and the Local Autonomy Law of 1947. There are three types of elections: general elections held every four years for the House of Representatives; elections held every three years for the House of Councillors; and local elections held every four years for offices in prefectures, cities and villages. All elections are on the basis of universal adult suffrage. The minimum voting age is 20, with a three-month residency requirement. For those seeking office, the minimum age is 25 for the House of Representatives and local legislative bodies and 30 for the House of Councillors. Elections are supervised by election committees at each administrative level under the general direction of the Central Election Administration Committee. The central committee is appointed by the prime minister on the advice of the Diet, while local committees are selected by the local assemblies.

In each of the 130 electoral districts, the successful candidates are those who win at least the fifth-largest aggregation of votes in a five-man district, the fourth-largest in a four-man district or the third-largest in a three-man district. Voters cast their ballots for one candidate only. In the House of Councillors elections, the 47 prefectural constituencies, including Tokyo and Hokkaido, elect from two to eight councillors, depending on their population, and each voter also casts one ballot for a candidate in the national constituency. The purpose of a national constituency is to have a nongeographical basis of representation for persons of outstanding talent or reputation who could serve as spokespersons for national interests.

The apportionment of election districts reflects the structure of population in the years just after World War II, when only one-third of the people lived in urban areas. Although the proportion has since shifted to 78% urban and 22% rural, no reform of the districts has been undertaken, resulting in glaring inequities. In urban districts four times as many votes are needed to elect a candidate as in rural districts. Despite a Supreme Court decision in 1976 declaring unconstitutional the allocation of lower house seats because it violated the principle of equal representation, no reform has been forthcoming because rural overrepresentation favors the ruling Liberal Democratic Party.

Another criticism leveled against the electoral system is that candidates are promoted by vast financial interests. Running for a Diet seat is expensive, and most candidates are underwritten by a complex network of interests and obligations and also wealthy factional bosses. Such support is expected to be repaid over a parliamentary term in various services, although this does not imply that all Japanese politicians are necessarily corrupt. Nevertheless, the relationship between the Diet member and his financial patron is a direct and exacting one, while that between the Diet member and the voter is an indirect and unquantifiable one.

The Election Law places limits on expenditures and campaign practices. Door-to-door canvassing is prohibited; only one campaign vehicle per candidate is permitted, and serving food or beverages as part of the campaign also is illegal. The numbers of mailings, posters, speeches and media appearances are all strictly limited. Candidates cannot buy television time during the campaign. Instead, the Election Law provides for each candidate to make three television appearances of four and a half minutes each, free of charge. These legal restrictions are generally circumvented by all candidates through typically ingenious means. Nevertheless, legal campaigning is relatively dull and colorless. However, since these restrictions apply only to the official campaign time, most of the real campaigning takes place before that time, stretching, in some cases, for months.

PARTY COMPOSITION IN THE DIET

House of Representatives (1986)

Party	Votes	% of Votes	Seats
Liberal Democratic Party	29,875,496	49.42	304
Japan Socialist Party	10,412,583	17.23	86
Komeito	5,701,277	9.43	57
Japanese Communist Party	5,313,246	8.79	27
Democratic Socialist Party	3,895,927	6.45	26
New Liberal Club	1,114,800	1.84	6
Social Democratic Federation	499,670	0.83	4
Other parties	120,627	0.20	—
Independents	3,515,042	5.81	2
Total	60,448,668	100.00	512

POLITICAL PARTIES

The Japanese party system has been characterized as the one-and-one-half party system, referring to the fact that it consists of the Liberal Democratic Party as the only full party in power continuously since 1948, and all other parties as the half party permanently in opposition. This does not imply that Japan does not have a lively and vigorous party system. When the 1947 Constitution

HOUSE OF COUNCILLORS (1986)	
Party	Seats
Liberal Democratic Party	142
Japan Socialist Party	41
Komeito	25
Japanese Communist Party	16
Democratic Socialist Party	12
New Liberal Club	2
Second Chamber Club	3
Salaried Workers' Party	3
Tax Party	2
Social Democratic Federation	1
Independents	4
Others	–
Vacant	1
TOTAL	252

came into effect, Japan had already had more than half a century of experience with political parties, although in a much muted form. It was only in the 1930s that left-wing parties were declared illegal and in 1940 that the remaining parties agreed to disband themselves into a fascist front, the Imperial Ruler Assistance Association.

Political parties are legally established and regulated in accordance with the Political Finance Control Law. The law imposes no ideological, ethnic or religious criteria. Party labels are less important than the broad political categories under which their programs are perceived by voters: conservative or progressive. As long as members do not cross this ideological line, they enjoy a certain flexibility in party affiliation. Moreover, with the exception of extreme left-wing and extreme right-wing parties, the focus of loyalty is not so much the party as the faction within a party *(habatsu)*. Factions are important as leavening elements within a party, inhibiting its growth as a monolithic organization. Factionalism *(batsu)* is rooted in Japanese history and extends to every area of national life: *zaibatsu* (commerce, industry and finance), *gumbatsu* (military), *kambatsu* (civilian bureaucracy) and *gakubatsu* (school or university), not to overlook the most important of all, *keibatsu* (family). Factionalism also is encouraged by the existing multimember, single-vote electoral system, which pits candidates from any one party against each other as much or even more than it pits them against opposition-party candidates. Thus political parties are essentially coalitions in themselves.

The Liberal Democratic Party (LDP) is Japan's most important and oldest party, tracing its roots to groups formed by Itagaki Taisuke and Okuma

Shigenobu in the 1880s. It attained its present form in 1955, when the conservative Liberal and Democratic parties joined in response to the threat posed by the unified Socialist Party. The LDP has been continuously in power since 1948, and its dominance may not be challenged in the foreseeable future.

The LDP is not, unlike the leftist parties, based upon a well-defined ideology or political philosophy, and sometimes its principles are difficult to define. Its members hold a variety of positions on the political spectrum between extreme right and center. Being in power for over 40 years, the LDP has been able to pursue and achieve a number of national goals, including rapid economic growth, close cooperation with the United States and efficient administration. The LDP's political power rests on a tripod of farmers, big businessmen, bureaucrats and traditional conservatives, thus encompassing all the traditional bastions of power in Japanese society. The LDP is characterized as the most traditional party in Japan, relying as it does not on ideological bonds but on the ancient patron-client *(oyabun-kobun)* relationship at both the national and local levels. Even within factions there are support groups *(koenkai)* engaged in mutual horse-trading. Success in the party is based on three factors: *jiban* (a strong, well-organized constituency), *kaban* (a briefcaseful of money) and *kanban* (a prestigious appointment, usually a ministry).

It is a cliché that the LDP is more a coalition of factions than a party. It is compared to a river into which many tributaries flow, but unlike the metaphor, each tributary maintains its own separate identity. Over the years factions have numbered from eight to 13, each with as few as four members or as many as 100. Faction leaders are the modern equivalents of the medieval *daimyos*, and each runs a virtual fiefdom and provides largess to the loyal followers, financial support during elections and introductions to influential people in the bureaucracy and the business world. During lulls in the constant infighting, temporary alliances are formed. Especially when a new prime minister is about to be chosen, a balance of power is struck between those who support him (the mainstream) and those who do not (the antimainstream). The spoils of the mainstream are the most prestigious cabinet ministries, such as those of finance, foreign affairs, and international trade and industry, while the antimainstream factions get the smaller crumbs. The intraparty bickering, although often sordid, has served a positive purpose. It has kept the party from ossifying and has encouraged challenges to party leadership. The challenges, however, are on personal rather than ideological grounds. There have been a few ideological groups within the LDP, of which the most prominent is the "Summer Storm Group" (Seirankei), formed in 1973; this group is rightist and critical of old-style faction politics. An effort during the 1970s to downgrade factions by introducing primaries for electing party leaders only intensified intraparty squabbles.

One of the factors contributing to factionalism in the LDP is *seiji shikin* (political funds) or, more crudely, *o-kane* (money). Although the party is one of the wealthiest in the world, its funds are divided among the factions and are insufficient to meet the expenses of maintaining an extensive establishment. From 1961 to 1975 the principal source of funds was the National Association (Kokumin Kyokai), through which laundered funds reached party coffers from rich corporations. Implicated in the Lockheed/Tanaka scandals in the early 1970s, it was replaced by the National Political Association (Kokumin Seiji Kyokai) with identical functions and staff. The amount of money a faction leader has influences the size of his following, and this size, in turn, influences the degree of power he is able to wield. However, the larger the number, the greater the demand on his financial resources. It has been maintained that the optimum factional size is 25 because, beyond this point, large factions tend to develop subfactions. However, most prime ministers in recent times have been factional leaders commanding the allegiance of more than 40 members.

Sometimes even mainstream factions are likely to disintegrate over dissatisfaction over allocation of cabinet seats and occasional differences over policy. Thus antimainstreamers are always waiting in the wings to work their way into power when this happens. LDP factional politics is thus reminiscent of medieval Japan's leadership—cautious and carefully hedged and constantly wary of being supplanted.

Leader	LDP FACTIONS House of Representatives	House of Councillors
Suzuki Zenko	52	29
Nikkaido Susumu*	65	53
Fukuda Takeo	47	25
Nakasone Yasuhiro	49	16
Komoto Toshio	26	12

*Surrogate for Kakuei Tanaka, the de facto factional head and former prime minister indicted in the Lockheed scandal.

The Japan Socialist Party (JSP) is descended from the prewar Socialist Party, which was formally organized in 1925. The JSP's brightest hour came with the Allied Occupation, when the labor union movement was greatly strengthened. They were briefly in power for nine months, from May 1947 to February 1948, under a coalition cabinet led by socialist veteran Tetsu Katayama. The present JSP was established in 1955 through the amalgamation of several socialist parties. Factionalism also is a fact of life for the Socialists, who are perhaps more badly split than the LDP. Of the three major JSP factions, two are moderate and one is militantly Marxist, and intraparty doctrinal disputes are intense and bitter. Often described as the political arm of the national labor federation, the Sohyo, JSP receives most of its finances and organizational support from trade unions. Since the 1950s the party has regularly garnered one-sixth of the national vote at every election but has not been able to break this barrier, and its goal of wresting power from the conservatives remains a distant one. The JSP's platform follows the classic socialist positions: nationalization of major industries, abolition of the military, abolition of entrance examinations for high school and college, opposition to constitutional revision and a neutral foreign policy.

There are two minor parties to the extreme left and extreme right: the Japan Communist Party (JCP) and the Komeito. The JCP, organized in 1922 in the wake of the Russian Revolution, remained an illegal party until 1945, and since then its fortunes have fluctuated from a high of 9.7% in 1949 to 2.6% in 1952 and from 39 seats in 1949 to five in 1963. Since the 1960s the party has been divided on the Sino-Soviet dispute. A formal break with Moscow took place in 1963, and the party drew closer to Beijing, only to break with the Chinese Communists in 1965. Since then the JCP has followed an independent line, stressing themes such as the parliamentary road of nonviolent electoral politics, quality of life, and neutrality in East-West rivalry. The Komeito, translated somewhat inaccurately as the Clean Government Party, is an offshoot of the militant Soka Gokkai (Value Creation Society), an organization of lay followers of Nichiren Buddhism. In 1970 it severed all ties with the Soka Gokkai, but its programs have a pro-Buddhist bias.

The Democratic Socialist Party was founded in 1960 by right-wing members of the Socialist Party led by Suehiro Nishio. Its policies represent a hodgepodge of LDP and JSP platforms.

The *Asahi Yearbook* reports that there are over 35,000 members of new left organizations organized into five major currents and 23 different factions as well as several thousand more persons in 300 or more anarchist groups, including some 11 radical student groups with picturesque names. The most conspicuous of these is the Red Army Faction formed in 1960 and which, like its namesake in Western Europe, is a terrorist group with few ideological pretensions. Right-wing groups are more diverse. There are reportedly over 600 of them, linked by a common desire to restore the glories of Meiji and Tokugawa Japan, particularly the divinity of the emperor.

ECONOMY

Japan is the third-richest country in the world, with a GNP half that of the United States and a per capita GNP equal to that of the United States. This is no mean achievement for a densely populated nation living in a relatively small national territory with little or no natural resources. Because economic growth rates in excess of 11% per year were attained in the postwar period, the gap between Japan and the major industrial economies was closed in a remarkably short time.

Rapid growth and structural flexibility have characterized Japan's economic development since the Meiji Restoration. Modern industry began to expand substantially in 1904. The share of industry equaled that of agriculture by the 1920s and overtook it thereafter. Most industrial growth, however, was geared toward the nation's military power, which was engulfed and devastated in World War II. It was not until the 1950s that the economy reached prewar levels. By then the Japanese economy, unencumbered by military imperatives, was on a fast track. In the 1960s and early 1970s Japan had some of the highest economic growth rates in the world, close to 12% annually. By the early 1970s the Japanese and the rest of the world were beginning to realize that Japan's prosperity was not a temporary or fragile phenomenon. As analysts began to err in the opposite direction of assuming that Japan's economy was on a limitless curve of endless growth, the country suffered its first real postwar recession in 1974, one combined with very high inflation. Nevertheless, Japan emerged from the first oil shock relatively unscathed and resumed its growth trajectory. Since 1974 Japan has not suffered a recession, but average annual growth has been slower than before. The average growth rate for the 1974–85 period was 4.3%, which was less than half the rate that prevailed during the previous 20-year period, even though the Japanese still outdistanced all other OECD members. The new era is called *anti seicho* (stable growth).

The reasons for Japan's economic success are complex and numerous. Institutional factors have played an important role in triggering and sustaining growth. Among the more important is the high level of investment, which persists even in the 1980s. Investment in capital equipment averages over 30% of the GNP, compared to 11% in the prewar period. The quality of investment also is critical to the economy's performance. As a latecomer to modernization, Japan was able to avoid some of the trial and error needed to perfect industrial processes. Well into the 1980s technology licensing, patent purchases, and imitation and improvement of foreign inventions were important. The technological gap between Japan and the other developed countries closed rapidly by the 1980s, and thereafter Japan emerged as an innovator. By the end of the 1980s Japan has become the acknowledged leader in a number of fields, including iron and steel, dynamic random-access memory, memory chips and automobiles. The end of the catch-up process is evidenced by the higher expenditures on research and development, estimated at close to 3% of GNP in 1987.

Third, Japan has one of the strongest Gross National Savings rates in the world. This is important because the government has chosen not to borrow heavily in the foreign market to finance domestic investment. Fourth, Japan has been politically stable since the war, with a popularly elected, noncoercive government. The economic policies are stable, less subject to shifts and changes, as power has been concentrated in the hands of a probusiness political party. The government provides supportive economic policies. At the macroeconomic level it has followed a tight fiscal policy and an expansionary monetary policy. It maintained a balanced budget until the mid-1960s, thus avoiding competition with the private sector for use of domestic savings. Further, public works spending is skewed toward industrially useful investment rather than social amenities. Interest rates are kept low, and money supply is permitted to expand rapidly. At the microeconomic level, the government imposed high import barriers to protect infant industries. Labor-management relations are nonconfrontational, and in general unions have been flexible on wages and work rules. Salary increases have been kept within the range of productivity gains. In addition, the Japanese worker is well educated by world standards, and his educational attainments have consistently surpassed the needs of the economy.

The economy entered a lower growth mode in the 1980s after the second oil shock. Capital formation slowed, technological innovation became more expensive, energy costs soared, the labor market shrank in response to slower population growth and decrease in hours worked, and gains in productivity slipped significantly. There also was a shift in priorities away from economic growth per se to a broader set of social goals.

Although Japan is for all practical purposes a free-market economy, the influence of the government is so pervasive that it has given rise to the phrase "Japan, Inc." The strategy of industrial growth and the allocation of investment funds are guided by the government. While the government's statutory powers to control business are less extensive than in most industrial nations, its nonstatutory powers are enormous. Most large corporations cultivate a patron-client relationship with one or more government ministries. The hand of the government is everywhere; ministries engage in consultation, advice, persuasion and threats. They set sectoral targets and plans. At the same time, large corporations have an equally enormous influence in channeling official policy into areas that best serve their interests. The influence of big business over government policy is exerted not only by individual firms but also through numerous joint committees and through national associations, of which Keidenren, is the most important. Both the public and the private sectors have important means of persuasion without resorting to formal measures of control.

Planning was introduced in the 1950s through a body known first as the Economic Stabilization Board and later as the Economic Planning Agency. The status of these plans remains ambiguous because they are based on estimates and goals rather than firm data and targets. The most striking fact about them was that actual performance of the plans to date has far exceeded the predictions.

Historically large monopolies and cartels known as *zaibatsu* played a dominant role in the economy, until they were dissolved under the Allied Occupation. It was followed by the passing of an antimonopoly law establishing the Fair Trade Commission. Its function is to ensure the existence of competitive conditions and prevent the reemergence of large, single-firm monopolies. It is empowered to eliminate substantial disparities in economic power, if necessary by divestiture, and to dismantle such monopoly devices as interlocking directorates, intercorporate stockholding and holding companies. Similarly, the Trade Association Act prohibits groups of firms from engaging in restrictive practices. As soon as the Occupation ended, the cartels returned as the *keiretsu* (multiple-firm oligopolies) for dumping goods in foreign markets and maintaining prices at home. A series of amendments to the anticartel laws reinstated former practices such as resale price maintenance. Special enactments sponsored by the Ministry of International Trade & Industry (MITI) made it possible for particular industries to bypass the law. Moreover, firms brought under the commission's scrutiny sometimes pleaded successfully that they had acted under "administrative guidance." Nevertheless, the influence of small and medium-size firms and consumers is sufficiently strong to prevent the total destruction of Fair Trade Commission and its antimonopolistic programs. According to the law, corporations engaging in unauthorized price cartels receive severe penalties. The commission also is empowered to break up an enterprise whose market share exceeds 50% of the industry. Two corporations that control over 75% of a market also are designated as monopolies and subject to antimonopoly regulations.

Each ministry and agency has the right to utilize "administrative guidance" in the area of its charter. Of these, MITI is by far the most active. MITI helps industry to form production cartels, explore new types of technology and adjust marketing strategies. Industrial cartels are of three different kinds. Recession cartels are formed when conditions in a particular industry have reduced prices below average production costs and threaten the survival of a significant number of producers. Rationalization cartels are permitted to improve the technical efficiency and product quality of an industry by limiting the use of a particular technology or product line. Guidance cartels are organized to advise industries of desirable levels of output, prices and investment. Other cartels may be formed by special Diet legislation. FTC approval is not necessary for such special cartels, and thus they are the most numerous.

The other major type of MITI involvement in the industrial structure is in mergers. Mergers have to be approved by the FTC, but compliance is voluntary. However, such is the power of MITI that the FTC seldom refuses its requests. Further, unless an enterprise is particularly powerful, it cannot afford to ignore MITI guidance. Before the liberalization of foreign trade in the 1960s, MITI used its control over the issuance of foreign exchange licenses as a means of persuading private industry to bend to its will. Although the ministry has lost some of its authority over particular types of economic activity, maintaining good relations, with the appropriate department of MITI is an important ingredient for business success.

A number of semigovernment advisory councils, committees or boards facilitate dialogue between government and business. There are over 85 such committees attached to various ministries and their departments, including the Economic Council, attached to the Economic Planning Agency; the Industrial Structure Council; and the Transportation Council. In addition, key business lobby groups serve as links between the government and the major sectors of the economy. The four national ones are the Federation of Economic Organizations (Keidanren), the Japanese Federation of Employers' Associations (Nikkeiren), the Committee for Economic Development (Keizai Doyukai) and the Japan Chamber of Commerce and Industry (Nissho). Keidanren, the most important of the four, includes in its membership the largest corporations and manufacturers' associations. Its advice on policy issues is regularly sought by the cabinet. Nikkeiren is largely concerned with labor-management relations. Keizai Doyukai concerns itself with the social responsibilities of big business. Nissho, the oldest, represents small and medium-scale businesses.

Japan's public corporations are unique features of an otherwise wholly private enterprise economy. In 1988 there were 97 such corporations, reduced from 111 as a result of administrative reforms. Those at the national level are normally affiliated with one of the economic ministries, although the extent of direct state management and supervision varies. Public corporations are divided into six categories. The *kosha* comprise the three main public service and monopoly corporations: Nippon Telegraph and Telephone, Japanese National Railways and Japan Tobacco and Salt, which together own a high proportion of the assets of public concerns. The *kodan*, public bodies that do not operate any service or industry but promote various types of constructional works, include the Japan Housing Corporation, the Japan Petroleum Development Corporation and the Japan Highways Corporation. The *koko* are development corporations financing various projects of national importance. The *kinko* are public financial corporations and include *ginko* (banks), such as the Bank of Japan. Besides these wholly public bodies, the government shares with private enterprise the ownership and management of several undertakings collectively known as *tokushu gaisha*. Finally, there are *jigyodan* semipublic bodies that are responsible for administering various public policies, including labor welfare, sugar price stabilization, coal mine area rehabilitation and livestock industry promotion. Theoretically these public corporations are self-financing, except for Japanese National Railways, which has suffered from chronic deficits. They also provide employment for retired bureaucrats, a process known as *amakudari* (descent from heaven). Like public corporations in other countries, they tend to be less efficient than those in the private sector and subject to frequent labor troubles and strikes.

Industrial development has given rise to regional problems that have resisted government reforms. The rapid industrialization of the 1950s and 1960s resulted in growth being concentrated in a narrow belt of land that stretches from the eastern part of Kanto to the northern part of Kyushu. Three conurbations and their satellite area within this zone—Tokyo-Yokohama (Kanto), Kyoto-Osaka-Kobe (Kinki) and Nagoya (Tokai)—are responsible for three-quarters of the industrial output and nearly half of the population. The Income Doubling Plan of 1961–70 was the first effort to reduce regional imbalances in population and income, and its Regional Development Program had as its main goal the diversion of industries to areas where labor, land and water are less scarce, such as Hokkaido, Tohoku, Shikoku and Chugoku-Kyushu. The failure of this program was followed by Prime Minister Tanaka's ambitious plan for the redevelopment of the Japanese archipelago, which included lavish public spending on the development of inland industrial parks and rail and road connections. The plan was discredited along with its author, but by the mid-1970s natural market forces began to operate where the planners had failed. Pollution, high land values and other factors helped to push the population outside the major conurbations, and the regions began to experience a modest growth.

The social and environmental costs of explosive industrial growth have been heavy. Until the mid-1970s the public and private sectors pursued economic growth with such single-mindedness that prosperity was accompanied by severe degradation of both the environment and the quality of life. A series of incidents—including *itai-itai* caused by severe cadmium poisoning and the Minamata poisoning from mercury, which deformed hundreds of people—caused a public outrage and led to new antipollution legislation and the eventual creation of an environmental agency. Increased expenditures on environmental programs have brought about a significant and visible improvement in environmental quality. Gaps in social amenities also received greater government attention in the 1980s. More public investment was diverted to social amenities such as roads, traffic safety and housing.

In 1986 the Japanese economy grew by 2.4% in real terms, the lowest rate of growth since 1974. The current account surplus and the merchandise trade surplus increased to $85.8 billion and $92.8 billion, respectively. From September 1985 to May 1987 the yen's value relative to the dollar rose from about 240 to 140. The positive effects of a strong yen, increasing Japan's purchasing power through declines in import prices, more than offset its deflationary impact. Thus the strong yen contributed to both reducing the external imbalance and stimulating domestic demand. It also helped to expand Japan's trade surplus with the United States to $58.6 billion in 1986. One objective of rate adjustments is to transform Japan's export-driven economic structure to one more dependent on domestic demand. To smooth such a transition, Japan is striving for a 4% annual real GNP growth, to achieve which domestic demand has to grow by more than 5% per year.

The 1986 foreign exchange adjustment, in which the yen appreciated 41.5% over the dollar, is bound to influence patterns of growth well into the 1990s. The nation's terms of trade improved by 38.1% in 1986 over the previous year. The strong yen, even while reducing the physical volume of exports and yen-denominated export income, has brought about large foreign exchange windfall profits. A rough estimate is that Japanese imports in 1986 were $62.9 billion cheaper as a result of the appreciation. If gains generated by the decline in world prices of crude oil are added, the savings to Japan exceeded $71.4 billion in 1986 alone. The benefits of the strong yen have not been passed through to Japanese workers and consumers in the form of wage hikes and price declines. The complicated distribution systems and oligopolistic marketeers have absorbed most of the benefits from the decline in import prices. In fact, import restrictions and price controls on agricultural and other products have kept the price of food much higher than in other countries. For example, the price of beef is three times as high and the price of rice four times as high as in the United States.

Despite the appreciation in the yen's value, Japan's current account and merchandise trade account surpluses in 1986 grew to $85.8 billion and $92.8 billion, respectively. Two major factors in this increase are the so-called J-curve effect of the exchange rate adjustment and the decline in crude oil prices. In the long-term capital account, Japan registered a $131.5 billion net capital outflow in 1986, compared to $15 billion in 1982. Japan has been reinvesting its massive merchandise trade surplus in foreign securities, real estate and other assets. Japan's net acquisition of foreign bonds, mostly dollar-denominated, totaled $93 billion and net direct investment abroad $14 billion in 1986. As a result, net investment income grew to 9.5 billion in 1986, compared to 1.7 billion in 1983.

The traditional services trade deficit has been shrinking in proportion to the expansion in net investment income. Japan's net external assets reached $180.4 billion in 1986, making it the largest creditor nation in the world.

As part of its efforts to restructure the Japanese economy, the government in 1987 adopted "emergency economic measures," which consisted of $35.7 billion in public works projects as well as income tax reductions worth $7.1 billion. To open Japanese markets to foreign companies and products, the government is considering advisory councils' policy recommendations, such as the 1986 Maekawa Report. If the dollar continues to decline, Japan will experience lower growth for the rest of the 1980s or will be forced to implement a more expansionary domestic policy in which private domestic demand will carry most of the load for further growth.

PRINCIPAL ECONOMIC INDICATORS

Gross National Product: $1.559 trillion (1986)
GNP per capita: $12,850 (1986)
GNP average annual growth rate: 4.3% (1973–86)
GNP per capita average annual growth rate: 3.4% (1973–86)
Income distribution:
Average annual rate of inflation: 1.6% (1980–86)
Consumer Price Index: (1980=100)
　　All items: 115.2 (January 1988)
　　Food: 113.3 (January 1988)
Wholesale Price Index: 1980=100 87 (November 1987)
Average annual growth rate (1980–86) (%)
　　Public consumption: 3.1
　　Private consumption: 2.9
　　Gross domestic investment: 3.2

PUBLIC FINANCE

The Japanese fiscal year runs from April 1 through March 31.

The drafters of the Constitution considered the budget so vital that they devoted an entire chapter (Chapter 7) to it. The expenditure budget is prepared for each fiscal year by the Budget Bureau of the Ministry of Finance and is based on requests from government ministries and agencies. The Tax Bureau is responsible for adjusting tax schedules and estimating revenues.

The ministry also issues government bonds; controls government borrowing; and administers the Fiscal Investment and Loan Program, sometimes referred to as the second budget.

```
┌─────────────────────────────────────────────────────┐
│           BALANCE OF PAYMENTS 1987 ($ Billion)        │
│                                                       │
│  Current account balance: 85.96                       │
│  Merchandise exports: 224.59                          │
│  Merchandise imports: 128.20                          │
│  Trade balance: 96.39                                 │
│  Other goods, services & income +: 79.70              │
│  Other goods, services & income –: 85.44              │
│  Private unrequited transfers: 0.96                   │
│  Official unrequited transfers: 2.73                  │
│  Direct Investment: 18.61                             │
│  Portfolio Investment: 90.80                          │
│  Other Long-term Capital: 24.20                       │
│  Other Short-term Capital: 89.00                      │
│  Net Errors & Omissions: 3.55                         │
│  Counterpart Items: 0.06                              │
│  Exceptional Financing:                               │
│  Liabilities Constituting Foreign                     │
│     Authorities' Reserves:                            │
│  Total Change in Reserves: 38.44                      │
└─────────────────────────────────────────────────────┘
```

Three types of budgets are prepared for the approval of the Diet each year. The general account budget includes most of the basic expenditures of current governmental operations. Special account budgets, of which there are about 40, cover programs and institutions such as public enterprises, pension funds and public works projects financed from special taxes. Finally there are the budgets of the 15 major state enterprises, including the *kosha*. Although these budgets are approved before the start of each fiscal year, they usually are addended or revised with supplemental budgets. All estimates are completed by August 31 of the previous fiscal year. September and October usually are devoted to revising these estimates. The budget procedure is unique at this stage in the sense that most attempts are made to increase rather than decrease expenditures. A draft budget is ready by January, and deliberations within party circles and one or two cabinet meetings follow. In late January the budget goes to the House of Representatives and within five days to the House of Councillors.

Although government expenditures are smaller as a proportion of the GNP than in most other industrial countries, fiscal policy is not restrictive. Government fixed investments in infrastructure and loans to public and private enterprises are about 15% of the GNP. Loans from the Fiscal Investment and Loan Program, which are outside the general budget and funded primarily from postal savings, represent more than 20% of the general account budget, but their total effect on economic investment is not completely accounted for in the national income statistics. Taxes, representing 14% of the GNP in 1987, are low in comparison to other developed economies. Individual income and corpo-

```
┌─────────────────────────────────────────────────┐
│            GROSS DOMESTIC PRODUCT 1985            │
│                                                   │
│ GDP nominal (national currency): 316.115 trillion │
│ GDP real (national currency): 291.207 trillion    │
│ GDP per capita ($): 10 456                        │
│ Average annual growth rate of GDP 1980–88: 4.0%   │
│                                                   │
│ GDP by type of expenditure (%)                    │
│   Consumption                                     │
│     Private: 59                                   │
│     Government: 10                                │
│   Gross domestic investment: 29                   │
│   Gross domestic saving: 32                       │
│   Foreign trade                                   │
│     Exports: 17                                   │
│     Imports: 14                                   │
│                                                   │
│ Cost components of GDP (%)                        │
│   Net indirect taxes: 6                           │
│   Consumption of fixed capital: 14                │
│   Compensation of employees: 55                   │
│   Net operating surplus: 24                       │
│                                                   │
│ Sectoral origin of GDP (%)                        │
│   Primary                                         │
│     Agriculture: 3                                │
│     Mining:                                       │
│   Secondary                                       │
│     Manufacturing: 30                             │
│     Construction: 7                               │
│     Public utilities: 3                           │
│   Tertiary                                        │
│     Transportation & communications: 6            │
│     Trade: 14                                     │
│     Finance: 15                                   │
│     Other services: 19                            │
│     Government: 5                                 │
│                                                   │
│ Average annual sectoral growth rate, 1980–86 (%)  │
│   Agriculture: 1.0                                │
│   Industry: 5.0                                   │
│   Manufacturing: 7.8                              │
│   Services: 2.9                                   │
└─────────────────────────────────────────────────┘
```

rate taxes provide 67.4% of total revenues. Income taxes are graduated and progressive, and those in higher tax brackets are given smaller deductions and higher tax rates than those in lower ones. Many types of individual savings and welfare expenditures also are deductible. The structural features of the tax system are the tremendous elasticity of the individual income tax and the use of special tax measures to promote national economic objectives. The inequality of income distribution before taxes is roughly the same in Japan as it is in the

OFFICIAL DEVELOPMENT ASSISTANCE

In $ million

1965	1970	1975	1980	1982	1983	1984	1985	1986	1987
244	458	1,148	3,353	3,023	3,761	4,319	3,797	5,634	NA

As percentage of GNP

1965	1970	1975	1980	1982	1983	1984	1985	1986	1987
0.27	0.23	0.23	0.32	0.28	0.32	0.34	0.29	0.29	NA

United States. However, the tax system in Japan is only mildly progressive and therefore has little effect on the relative distribution of income after taxes. Because inheritance taxes and taxes on property income have been light, there has been increasing concentration of wealth in the upper tax brackets.

Japan had balanced budgets until 1966 because of a historic reluctance to resort to deficit spending. Budgetary deficits became a regular feature during the 1970s and reached a peak of Y11.2 trillion (5.5% of the GNP) in 1978. A policy of fiscal reconstruction was adopted in the early 1980s that limited growth in public expenditures to less than 1% per annum over the period 1980–85. As a result, deficit in the general account had declined to 3% of the GNP by 1987. The deficit of the local authorities was still smaller in 1987, at 0.3% of the GNP; further, there was a significant surplus in Social Security funds, equal to 29% of the GNP. The surplus reflects the relatively young population and the still immature pension system; as the population ages, the surplus will disappear. Central government bonds outstanding amount to nearly 50% of the GNP, and gross interest payments are 19.8% of total budget expenditures. A particular medium-term objective is the elimination of deficit-financing bonds by 1990.

The initial budget for 1987 sought to further financial reconstruction. However, the huge external surplus encouraged the government to increase public spending by an additional Y5 trillion and to reduce household taxes by Y1.83 trillion. These substantial measures of fiscal relaxation did not increase the budget, because of unusually rapid growth of tax revenues. The 1988 budget maintained the level of public works spending. It also brought down the rate of the deficit relative to the GNP and the rate of national bonds outstanding relative to the GNP. Stronger revenue growth and the proceeds from the sale of public sector assets have brought the government closer to its fiscal consolidation goals.

Tax reform remains under intensive discussion, although a comprehensive measure introduced by the government in 1987 failed to win the approval of the Diet because of opposition to a proposed tax similar to the VAT. The general objective of tax reform is to reduce the scale of direct taxation, which is high in comparison to other countries while at the same time reducing tax preferences now granted to specific activities, particularly savings.

CENTRAL GOVERNMENT EXPENDITURES, 1986
% of total expenditures

Defense: 6.5
Education: 9.0
Health: N.A.
Housing, Social Security, welfare: 18.7
Economic services: N.A.
Other: N.A.
Total expenditures as % of GNP: 17.4
Overall surplus or deficit as % of GNP: —4.9

CENTRAL GOVERNMENT REVENUES, 1986
% of total current revenues

Taxes on income, profit & capital gain: 67.4
Social Security contributions: 0.0
Domestic taxes on goods & services: 18.9
Taxes on international trade & transactions: 1.7
Other taxes: 7.5
Current nontax revenue: 4.6
Total current revenue as % of GNP: 12.6

Government consumption as % of GNP: 10 (1986)
Annual growth rate of government consumption: 3.1%
(1980–86)

GENERAL BUDGET ESTIMATES

('000 million yen, year ending 31 March)

Revenue	1985/86	1986/87	1987/88
Taxes and stamps	38,550	40,560	41,194
Public bonds	11,680	10,946	10,501
Others	2,270	2,583	2,406
Total	52,500	54,089	54,101

Expenditure	1985/86	1986/87	1987/88
Social security	9,574	9,835	10,090
Education and science . .	4,841	4,845	4,850
Government bond servic-			
ing	10,224	11,320	11,334
Defence	3,137	3,344	3,517
Public works	6,369	6,223	6.082
Local finance	9,690	10,185	10,184
Pensions	1,864	1,850	1,896
Total (incl. others)	52,500	54,089	54,101

CURRENCY & BANKING

The national currency is the yen (Y), divided into 100 sen, each sen being divided into 10 rin. Coins are issued in denominations of 1, 5, 10, 50 and 100 yen and notes in denominations of 500, 1,000, 5,000 and 10,000 yen.

The banking system is headed by the Bank of Japan (Nippon Ginko), founded in 1882 as the central bank. The bank's policy board consists of the bank governor, representatives from the Economic Planning Agency and the Ministry of Finance, and appointees from the private banking community. The board's decisions are effectively guided by the Banking Bureau of the Ministry of Finance. However, as Japanese banks are becoming less dependent on domestic credit than formerly, direct government control is slowly waning.

The Bank of Japan's main instruments for monetary control are its lending and discount policies, supplemented by what is known as "window guidance" (*madoguchi kisei*), which allows it to set quotas for lending. The central bank periodically adjusts the bank or discount rate — high during periods of monetary restraint and low during periods of expansion. Less important instruments of monetary control are reserve requirements and operations in the financial markets. The central bank determines the ratio of reserves to be desposited in it for all types of deposit institutions. The maximum reserve ratio allowed by law is 20%, but the actual requirements are much lower, typically less than 2%. Until the mid-1970s the central bank engaged in only limited forms of open market operations. The gradual liberalization of the financial system and the need for increased government borrowings, however, have caused the government to become increasingly active in marketing securities. Purchasing securities in the open market is thus another means of pumping money into the system.

Japan's financial system is geared toward providing industrial rather than consumer credit. About 90% of the nation's financial assets flows into the corporate and public sector through the banks, while only 6% goes through the stock market. The core of the banking system consists of 76 "commercial banks", divided into two categories: city banks (*tochi ginko*) and regional or local banks (*chiho ginko*). (The terms "commercial banks" and "trading banks" are not used in Japan.) The differences between the two are slightly confusing. As a rule, city banks have their head offices in large cities and operate on a national scale. They include Fuji Bank, Sumitomo Bank, Mitsubishi Bank, Sanwa Bank, Tokai Bank, Dai-Ichi Kangyo Bank, Mitsui Bank, Kyowa Bank, Daiwa Bank, Taiyo-Kobe Bank and Hokkaido Takushoku Bank. The Bank of Tokyo also is counted as one of the city banks, although legally it is a specialized foreign exchange bank. Regional banks operate mainly in limited local districts. It is also claimed that city banks are large and regional banks small. But there are exceptions to these definitions. There are some city banks with head offices in the same regional cities as regional banks, and some regional banks are equal in size to the city banks, although overall, regional banks have only one-tenth of the deposits of city banks. The real differences lie in the type of customers and the nature of the business. City banks lend more than half of their total loanable funds to large enterprises, and more than 60% of their deposits come from large corporations. Because of the heavy demands for investment funds, city banks are perpetually short of cash and in debt to the Bank of Japan and to the call-loan market. They are always "over borrowed" and particularly sensitive to monetary controls such as increases in the bank rate and window guidance.

Much of the long-term credit supply originates in the public banks, particularly the Long-Term Credit Bank of Japan and the Industrial Bank of Japan. These institutions are allowed to raise capital by issuing special debentures to other financial institutions. In the private sector, the seven trust banks are the primary sources of long-term capital. They are an amalgamation of private pension funds, unit trusts and mutual fund management groups who acquire extra funds by issuing loan trust certificates. Insurance companies also extend long-term loans to industry, while a host of mutual savings and loans, credit associations and cooperatives lend to medium and small-scale enterprises. The Japan Development Bank funds heavy industries and mining.

In the 1980s a total of 63 foreign banks operate in Japan and are licensed under the Bank Law to conduct domestic and foreign exchange transactions. The postal savings system *(yubin chokin seido)* competes with the seven trust banks for savings deposits from the general public and utilizes the vast network of 22,330 post offices. The total amount of postal savings is over 80% of total individual deposits in commercial and trust banks combined. These savings, together with surplus funds of special government accounts, are channeled to the Trust Funds Bureau. The foreign exchange banking business is handled by the Bank of Tokyo, all authorized foreign exchange banks, class A and B; and Tokyo branches of foreign banks. The agricultural sector is served by agricultural cooperative associations along with their credit federations, one in each prefecture, as well as the Central Cooperative Bank for Agriculture and Forestry. The Export-Import Bank of Japan borrows most of its funds from the government's Industrial Investment Special Account.

The Japanese banking industry is in the late 1980s the best-developed in the world. Of the 10 largest banks in the world, six are Japanese, including Dai-Ichi Kangyo, which is the No. 1 bank. The system is characterized by a number of factors. Japan's savings rate is perhaps the highest of any major country, accounting for about 20% of disposable income, compared to about 7% in the United States. Traditional thrift habits are reinforced by the fact that a large proportion of Japanese are self-employed. Further, the level of Social Security benefits are so low that this calls for greater individual saving effort, while the limited availability of housing and consumer credit has the same outcome. Among other positive factors are the large number of banking offices, amounting to one for every 10,000 Japanese, and the heavy promotion of savings by banks and corporations. The subdivision of demand deposits into three categories — ordinary deposits, notice deposits and current deposits — also has a healthy effect on the size of savings.

Japan's economy is less monetary than that of other industrial countries. The use of checks and giro transfers is less popular among the bulk of households, who still favor payment in currency. Further, Japanese monetary authorities focus their attention specifically on control of credit rather than on money. Credit is the lever by which the Bank of Japan effectively steers the economy. Again, the importance of credit is derived from some characteristic features of the financial system. Housing and consumer credit are the least favored sectors, and banks are principally channels for transferring massive surpluses to the corporate sector. In the absence of a strong capital market (until recently), corporate finance is heavily reliant on debt — a condition known in Japan as overborrowing. The ratio of equity to total capitalization is about 18% in Japan as compared to 51% in the United States. Such a low equity ratio carries substantial risks, especially during recessions when, because of "tenure commitments", companies cannot lay off workers. Additionally, the proportion of bond financing is low in relation to bank borrowing. Overborrowing is promoted by a number of factors, such as the intimacy between bankers and clients, the deductibility of interest, rapid external growth and the high costs of equity financing when new shares are issued at par value rather than at or near the market price. Thus Japanese corporations benefit from increasing their leverage by extensive bank borrowing. The resulting illiquidity of commercial banks is tolerated by monetary authorities, even though viewed with misgivings by orthodox financiers. Because the demand for loans exceeds the supply, it has been necessary to resort to qualitative controls over credit. The central bank uses two devices for this purpose. It sets limits on the amount it is prepared to lend at the lowest rate of interest, and it imposes higher or penalty rates on loans above that limit. By lowering or raising the ceiling it can control the supply of credit. The commercial banks follow the same practice in regard to their clients. The method is reinforced by window regulation, discriminating in favor of or against borrowers. Thus credit-granting decisions are brought to conformity with national economic policy.

As in other sectors, groups are characteristic of banking. Of the groups that are prominent today, several go back in their composition and methods of operation to the *zaibatsu* of pre-World War II days. These holding companies disappeared as a result of postwar reforms. But the largest of these groups, such as Mitsubishi, Mitsui and Sumitomo, were reconstituted under the leadership of the banks previously associated with these groups. Other banks assembled new groups around them. Group membership offers financial and nonfinancial advantages. The latter include joint sale and purchase arrangements, vertical integration, assured markets and sources of supply, technological affinity, combined research and cooperative planning. Attachment to a particular bank-led group means more than a line of credit. It means a commitment by the bank to protect the enterprise in all but the direst circumstances. Group membership does not guarantee credit, because firm credit lines of the U.S. variety do not exist in Japan. Loans from the group bank have the effect of improving the lopsided capital structure of Japanese enterprises. The activities of the bank as the leader of a group differ widely with respect to particular group members. Members cluster around the bank in concentric circles, with the bank's influence diminishing toward the periphery. If an enterprise gets into trouble, the bank might replace its management with delegates from its own senior staff. However, the relationship between groups and their banks is not exclusive. Banks lend to nongroup members, and members obtain loans from banks other than the group bank.

Beginning in the mid-1970s, the financial system experienced extensive liberalization and deregulation. The principal landmarks have been the decontrol of interest on large deposits in October 1985; the progressive reduction in the minimum size of such deposits; the opening of the system to foreign banks; the opening of the Tokyo Stock Exchange to foreign securities firms; the lifting of restrictions on the issue of Euroyen bonds; the liberalization of yen-denominated bond issues in Japan by nonresidents; and the opening of the Tokyo offshore market in 1986. These reforms have propelled Japan toward a more diverse and less tightly controlled system, offering investors and borrowers a broader range of options. Interest rates on many forms of investment have been deregulated, many more types of financial instruments have become available and the strict differentiation and segmentation of roles and responsibilities among the various financial institutions have been weakened. Awash with funds to invest and freed from the stringent regulations of the past, Tokyo has emerged as one of the largest and most important financial centers in the world.

Although Japan is not the only industrial country to undergo such rapid change, both the process of adjustment and the motivations for it have been very different from those elsewhere. Japan started with a more tightly controlled system, and one that had served the country well. Therefore, changes have not come easily, and government decisions have been cautious and incremental, characterized by extreme aversion to risk and the desire to distribute both the benefits and the burdens of liberalization fairly among all segments of the industry.

Prior to 1973, the financial system was characterized by an absence of a market for government bonds, preference for indirect rather than direct financing and a preference for direct controls in monetary policy. The government issued only short-term bills until 1966, and the long-term bonds issued after 1966 were carefully controlled with only one maturity: 10 years. The preference for indirect finance resulted from a number of reasons. During the 1960s, Japanese corporations raised 39% of their funds from bank loans, in contrast to 16% in the United States, and 2% in bonds, in contrast to 13% in the United States. The Japanese people preferred to deposit savings in banks instead of purchasing corporate stocks and bonds directly. In 1965 they held 93% of their financial portfolios in cash, demand deposits and time deposits, and only 7% in securities. The preference for bank deposits was reinforced by the lack of alternative financial instruments. There were no government bonds or short-term government securities, commercial paper, bankers' acceptances or negotiable certificates of deposits and few corporate bonds. Monetary policy used direct controls such as window guidance, which worked relatively well. In times of monetary restraint, when limits were tightened, the city banks turned more heavily to the call market, which spread the effects of the restraint more uniformly throughout the banking industry.

Although there were no serious bottlenecks in the smooth flow of capital to more productive uses, pressures began to appear making change imperative. Five of these pressures were technological change, slower economic growth, continued high savings, an aging population and foreign developments. Technological innovation facilitated the desire and the ability of the banking sector to respond efficiently to changing conditions. With the rise of government deficits after 1966, the government began to issue variable-maturity bonds at interest rates closer to the market rate. Resale of bonds to secondary markets was allowed from 1977. Short-term government securities were introduced in 1986 and soon claimed 26% of private sector purchases.

Changing corporate financial needs also helped to alter the financial system. Banks discovered that their strong dependence on loans to corporations was becoming a liability as the market stagnated. Further, corporations were turning from banks to the gensaki market and negotiable certificates of deposit (CD) for liquid, short-term investments. High rates of personal saving also brought important changes in financial behavior. Individuals became concerned with returns on their investments, but portfolio diversification remained modest and investment in corporate equities actually dropped, while those in postal savings and time deposits grew.

Although the market shares of the various types of financial institutions have not undergone dramatic changes in the postwar era, each type has strengths and weaknesses altered in the process of liberalization. Although the government is anxious to maintaining the balance among the various sectors of the banking industry, exposure to more intense competition and the removal of many regulatory barriers have brought changes in profitability. In general, city banks, trust banks and postal savings institutions have done well and expanded their business while agricultural and credit cooperatives, *shogo* (small regional mutual savings banks) and *shinkin* (very small local banks) banks have lost ground. In 1989 shogo banks ceased to exist as a separate category. There is some concern over the possibility of bank failures. Mergers and consolidations, such as the absorption of the failing Heiwa Sogo Bank by Sumitomo Bank, are considered part of bank strategy to meet the dislocations brought about by deregulation.

The *gensaki* (short-term lending market using repurchase agreements on government bonds) market was created in the early 1970s. The call market was split into a very short (overnight and seven-day) and a longer-term bill discount market. The next development came with the creation of negotiable certificates of deposit in 1979 and bankers' acceptances and money market certificates in 1985. These innovations were aimed at institutional participants rather than individuals. Japan still lacks treasury bills. There also is no commercial paper market.

Two types of pension funds operate, the first governed by rules established by the tax authorities and the second by the Ministry of Health and Welfare. The first is the *zaisei tekikaku nenkin seido* (tax-qualified retirement pension system). The second is the *chosei nenken* (adjusted pension that operates as an adjunct of the government's welfare pension fund). The first applies to any corporation with 20 or more employees, and the second to corporations with more than 1,000 employees. The smallest corporations have self-managed pension funds, which do not qualify for tax benefits. Closely related to the pension fund development has been the *tokutei kinsen shintaku*, or *tokkin* for short (portfolio management agreements in which a corporation establishes a trust account with a trust bank and enters into a contract with an investment advisory company to manage the portfolio). Both pension funds and *tokkin* have worked to the advantage of securities companies, since substantial portions of these funds are invested in corporate equities purchased on the stock market through securities firms.

Regulations regarding corporate bonds also have been liberalized. Unsecured bonds have been permitted since 1985, although with stringent balance sheet requirements. Unsecured yen-denominated bonds (called samurai bonds), formerly restricted to foreign governments and foreign-government-owned public utilities, have been permitted for foreign corporations. The strict segmentation of the banking sector has been gradually whittled away through a series of actions permitting banks and securities companies to create joint ventures.

These changes and adjustments have had serious implications for monetary policy. The government has been moving cautiously away from direct controls to indirect ones, through influencing interest rates or monetary aggregates. The discount rate is being increasingly used as an instrument. Another is the alteration of money supply and interest rates through purchases and sales of bonds, known in the United States as open market operations. By buying or selling in the bill discount market the Bank of Japan can raise or lower the cost of funds and thus affect lending activity.

Japan's securities market expanded rapidly in the 1980s. Between 1980 and 1985 the number of stock transactions on the Tokyo Stock Exchange rose from 100.219 billion to 118.205 billion, the value of transactions from Y35.403 trillion to Y75.453 trillion and the Nikkei Average Stock Price Index from Y6,870 to Y12,557. A substantial percentage of new equity financings on the Tokyo Stock Exchange are public offerings — i.e., not at par. Dividends are stable in amounts per share over considerable periods, and the payout rate is roughly constant by repeatedly issuing new stock at par. The global stock market crash of October 1987 affected the Tokyo Stock Exchange less than it did exchanges in Europe and North America. Prices on the Tokyo Stock Exchange fell by around 34% but rebounded to normal levels by 1988.

FINANCIAL INDICATORS, 1987

International reserves minus gold: $80.973 billion
  SDRs: 2463
    Reserve position in IMF: 2853
    Foreign exchange: $75.657 billion
Gold (million fine troy oz): 24.23

Central bank
  Assets
    Foreign assets: 23.4%
    Claims on government: 39.5%
    Claims on bank: 37.1%
    Claims on private sector: —
  Liabilities
    Reserve money: 112.2%
    Government deposits: 4.9%
    Foreign liabilities: —
    Capital accounts: —

FINANCIAL INDICATORS, 1987 *(continued)*

Money supply
Stock in trillion national currency: 98.214
M^1 per capita: 806.000
U.S. liabilities to: $115.462 billion
U.S. claims on: $95.905 billion

Private banks
  Assets
    Loans to government: 12.3%
    Loans to private sector: 78.3%
    Reserves: 1.3%
    Foreign assets: 8.1%
  Liabilities: deposits: Yen 445.358 trillion
    of which
    Demand deposits: 16.2%
    Savings deposits: 53.2%
    Government deposits: —
    Foreign liabilities: 13.4%

EXCHANGE RATE
Yen per U.S. dollar

1982	1983	1984	1985	1986	1987	1988
235	232	251	200.5	159.1	123.0	128.0

GROWTH PROFILE (Annual Growth Rates, %)

Population, 1985–2000: 0.5
Crude birth rate, 1985–90: 11.4
Crude death rate, 1985–90: 6.2
Urban population, 1980–85: 1.8
Labor force, 1985–2000: 0.5
GNP, 1973–86: 4.3
GNP per capita, 1973–86: 3.4
GDP, 1980–85: 4.0
Inflation, 1980–86: 1.6
Agriculture, 1980–86: 1.0
Industry, 1980–86: 5.0
Manufacturing, 1980–86: 7.8
Services, 1980–86: 2.9
Money holdings, 1980–86: 8.6
Manufacturing earnings per employee, 1980–85: 2.2
Energy production, 1980–86: 5.3
Energy consumption, 1980–86: 1.5
Exports, 1980–86: 11.5
Imports, 1980–86: 6.4
General government consumption, 1980–86: 3.1

(continued)

JAPAN'S FINANCIAL INSTITUTIONS

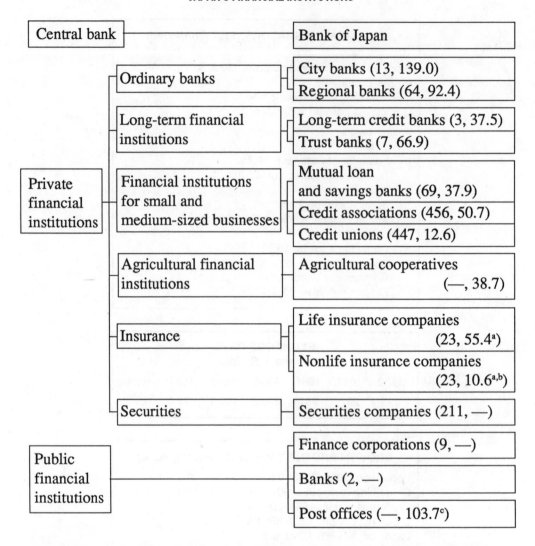

Source: Bank of Japan, *Keizai tokei geppo* (Economic Statistics Monthly), October 1986.

Note: Figures in parentheses show number of institutions and total of outstanding deposits and bond issues in trillions of yen as of June 1986.

a. Operating assets.
b. As of May 1986.
c. As of April 1986.

GROWTH PROFILE (Annual Growth Rates, %) *(continued)*
Private consumption, 1980–86: 2.9
Gross domestic investment, 1980–86: 3.2

AGRICULTURE

Japanese agriculture is very dissimilar to that of the rest of Asia in many respects and constitutes the weakest link in the economy. It has the highest use of mechanical power per hectare of cultivated land, the highest rate of use of chemical fertilizers and insecticides per hectare and one of the highest yields per hectare in the world. Its has some of the best-educated and most skilled farmers in the world. Technologically it is efficient, yet uneconomic in its present structure and income yield, particularly in relation to competing productive sectors. Although Japanese agriculture enjoys high protection from imports and a disproportionate share of government subsidies and price supports, the output per worker has not kept pace either with the population or with nonagricultural production. Self-sufficiency has been recorded only in vegetables, oranges and, to a lesser degree, rice. But the cost is very high to both the consumers and the taxpayers. The prices of essential foodstuffs such as wheat, barley and meat are three to seven times higher than those prevailing in comparable countries.

The most striking feature of Japanese agriculture is the shortage of farmland. The 4,996,000 ha. (12,340,120 ac.) being farmed constitute only 13.2% of the total land area. However, the land is intensively cultivated. It is estimated that 133% of the arable soil is under crops (i.e., an average of 1.33 crops are grown on every farm). The percentage varies with the region and according to the length of the growing season. In the subtropical regions of the Southwest it is 180%, dropping to 101% in Honshu and 85% to 98% in the colder Hokkaido. Rice fields occupy most of the countryside, whether on the alluvial plains, the terraced slopes or the swamplands and coastal bays. The varied aspects of the fields are due to their unequal shapes and also to the unequal length of time rice is given to mature, from eight months in the Southwest to only four in Hokkaido. The fields are irregular and small as the result of centuries of subdividing, but there are no fences.

The nonrice farmlands share the terraces and lower slopes and are planted with a variety of crops: wheat and barley in the autumn and sweet potatoes, vegetables and dry rice in the summer. Intercropping is common, and these crops alternate with beans and peas. South of Mount Fuji on the Pacific side and at Niigata on the Sea of Japan side, tea is grown in parallel rows extending over hills. Cultivation extends even to steep mountain slopes. Drought is a constant danger to overcome, and the land is crisscrossed by a latticed network of irrigation channels. Nearly all rice fields are flooded at the time of planting, and 75% of the water comes from rivers and lakes, 8% from springs or underground sources and 17% from rain catchments. Although rice will theoretically grow up to the northern limits of the country, climatic conditions inhibit the growth of most other crops in some regions. The central zone is the land of the rice paddy, where it is grown according to centuries-old intricate methods. Within this ancient zone there are variations according to climate. Only one crop per year is harvested on the northwestern coast of San-in and Hokuriku. On the Pacific coast rice is confined to the northern and central regions, leaving the plains for higher-priced crops such as mandarins, tea, vegetables and flowers, while the hills and plateaus are given over to pastureland for cattle. Along the Inland Sea and in certain parts of Kyushu, orchards and cattle farms outnumber the rice fields that once were supreme. Here hothouses are more numerous, agriculture is more commercialized and cooperatives are better organized. Around this rural heartland extends a peripheral zone with a subtropical climate where two rice crops are grown annually. It includes the southern end of the Kii Peninsula in Kansai, southern Shikoku (Kochi and Tokushima) and Kyushu (Miyazaki and Kagoshima). In northern Honshu the growing season is so short that north of Sendai the fields lie fallow all winter. In northern Tohoku, where production is higher than the national average, agriculture is primitive in the highlands, but in the plains the farmers are modern and prosperous. The average size of farms is highest in Hokkaido, where farming is highly mechanized and production extremely diversified.

Japanese agriculture has been characterized as a sick sector because it has to contend with a host of constraints, such as a rapidly diminishing labor suppy, the equally diminishing availability of arable land, and falling agricultural incomes. Nevertheless, production has been maintained at high levels since World War II through technical and administrative props. Technical advances have kept farming as a still viable industry through lavish use of fertilizers, use of farm machinery on a scale comparable to the United States and the increased use of vinyl plastics for market-garden plants to protect them against frost. The administrative props consist of extensive price supports and subsidies, which are not only straining the national budget but also are perpetuating production inefficiencies. The nation's 9,841 agricultural cooperatives are in charge of purchasing grain according to prices indexed to the average wage rates in the nonagricultural sector. As a result, rice, wheat and barley prices have followed productivity trends in industry rather than in agriculture. This type of support system, enacted in 1960 along with the Basic Agricultural Law, has resulted in large government rice stockpiles and ridiculously high agricultural prices. Even a major rice crop failure in 1980 failed to reduce the accumulated stocks by more than a quarter of the total reserves.

Two other goals of the government's agricultural policy are the promotion of consolidation of holdings, and the shift from rice to other crops, such as soybean, feed grain and wheat. Nevertheless, the structure of production favors rice. Production of rice is 12 times that of other grains and its self-sufficiency over 10 times that of others.

One significant trend in farming is the growing proportion of part-time farmers, defined as those whose total income is only partially derived from agriculture. On this basis, farming is a part-time and casual occupation for four-fifths of those described as farmers. A worse prognosis for the sector is that in all full-time farm households, the elderly predominate, revealing a loss of interest in farming among the younger generation. There is, as a result, a reluctance to make large-scale capital investment in land and machinery. Where farm help is scarce, the second or winter crop is not sown and generally the farm is more neglected.

Japan has had two land reforms since the Meiji Restoration. One was at the time of the restoration, when the feudal land rights were abolished in return for government compensation in the form of bonds. At that time, the de facto owners of land became de jure owners as well. However, the tenants did not receive any increased rights to their land. Indeed, when the Civil Code was later passed, tenants generally lost their former security of tenure.

A second and a more radical reform came only after the end of World War II, when the Occupation authorities pushed the Revised Farmland Adjustment Law of 1946 and the Owner-Farmer Establishment Law of 1946. This reform virtually wiped out land tenancy by making the vast majority of tenants the owners of the land they leased. The four main features of the reform were compulsory purchase by the government of some land and its resale to peasants, establishment of limits on the future acquisition of land by farmers, fixing extremely low rents on the remaining tenanted land and giving tenants virtually absolute security of tenure.

Livestock raising is a minor activity. Although the number of dairy cattle is increasing, the difficulty of securing animal feeds, most of which have to be imported, has made the expansion of beef cattle raising slow. Domestic beef production meets about 70% of the demand. Milk cows are numerous in Hokkaido, where 25% of the farmers are dairymen, but milk cows also are raised in Iwate, in Tohoku and near Tokyo and Kobe. Beef cattle are concentrated in the West, in Hiroshima and Kyushu, where one-third of the total number are found on the southern slopes. Hogs are the oldest domesticated animals in Japan and are found everywhere. Pork is the most popular meat.

The nation's forest resources, although abundant, are not well suited to sustaining a large lumber industry. Of the 24.5 million ha. (60.5 million ac.) of forests, 19.8 million ha. (48.9 million ac.) are classified as active forests. Often forestry is a part-time activity for farmers or small companies. About a third of all forests are owned by the government. Production is highest in Hokkaido and in the Aomori, Iwate, Akita, Fukushima, Gifu, Miyazaki and Kagoshima prefectures.

Japan is the world's second-largest fishing nation and the largest in per capita terms. Until the late 1970s the fastest-growing and largest share of the total annual catch came from deep-sea fisheries, for which the nation had built up a fleet of over 370,000 gross tons, including factory ships and trawlers. However, since the enactment of the 322-km. (200-mi.) exclusive economic zone around most of the world's coastal nations in the late 1970s, Japan's deep-sea catch has tapered off, and the fleet has been reduced to less than 300,000 gross tons. Japan also is one of the world's few whaling nations. As a member of the International Whaling Commission, the government has pledged that its fleets would restrict their catch to international quotas but has earned much opprobrium for failing to sign an agreement placing a moratorium on sperm whaling. The industry is in the hands of a few big companies. There are over 2,000 fishing ports, including Nagasaki, in southern Kyushu; Otaru, Kushiro and Abashiri in Hokkaido; and Yaezu and Misaki on the Pacific littoral.

AGRICULTURAL INDICATORS 1986

Agriculture's share of GDP: 3.0%
Average annual growth rate: 1.0% (1980–86)
Value added in agriculture: $61.550 billion
Cereal imports (000 tons): 27,119
Index of Agricultural Production: 1979–81=100 108.5
    (1985)
Index of Food Production 1979–81=100: 110.4 (1985):
    108 (1984–86)
Index food production per capita: (1979–81=100)
Number of tractors: 1,095,700
Number of harvester-threshers: 916,300
Total fertilizer consumption: 1,879,000 tons
Fertilizer consumption per ha.: 100 grams 4,273
Number of farms: 4,376,000
Average size of holding, ha. (ac.): 1.2 (2.9)
Size class (%)
    Below 1 ha. (below 2.47 ac.): 69.9
    1–5 ha. (2.47–12.35 ac.): 28.4
    5–10 ha. (12.35–24.7 ac.): 1.7
    10–20 ha. (24.7–49.4 ac.): 1.7
    20–50 ha. (49.4–123.5 ac.): 1.7
    50–over 200 ha. (123.5–494 ac.): 1.7

```
┌─────────────────────────────────────────────────┐
│      AGRICULTURAL INDICATORS 1986 (continued)     │
│   Over 200 ha. (over 494 ac.): 1.7                │
│ Tenure (%):                                       │
│   Owner-operated: 79.4                            │
│   Rented: —                                       │
│   Other: 20.6                                     │
│ Activity (%):                                     │
│   Mainly crops: 80.8                              │
│   Mainly livestock: 19.2                          │
│   Mixed: 19.2                                     │
│ % of farms using irrigation: 67                   │
│   Total farmland: 4,996,000 ha.                   │
│ Farms as % of total land area: 13.2               │
│ Land use (%): Cropland: 86.4                      │
│     Permanent crops: 10.9                         │
│     Temporary crops: 84.8                         │
│     Fallow: 4.3                                   │
│   Meadows & pastures: 13.6                        │
│   Woodland: —                                     │
│   Other: —                                        │
│ Yields kg/ha (lb./ac.)                            │
│   Grains: 5,898                                   │
│   Roots & tubers: 24,931                          │
│   Pulses: 1,641                                   │
│   Milk, kg./animal: 5,000                         │
│ Livestock (000)                                   │
│   Cattle: 4,742                                   │
│   Horses: 23                                      │
│   Sheep: 26                                       │
│   Pigs: 11,061                                    │
│ Forestry                                          │
│   Production of roundwood: 33,465,000 cub meters  │
│     of which industrial roundwood (%): 98.4       │
│   Value of exports ($000): 770,543                │
│ Fishing                                           │
│   Total catch (000 tons): 11,443.7                │
│     of which marine (%): 98.2                      │
│ Value of exports ($000): 819,840                  │
└─────────────────────────────────────────────────┘
```

MANUFACTURING

Few countries have pursued industrial growth so relentlessly as Japan, and fewer have achieved such notable success within such a short span. At the end of World War II Japan was an underdeveloped nation, with her industries laid low and with few exportable products other than ancient handicrafts. By the

1980s Japan had overtaken West Germany to become the world's second-largest industrial nation and one whose exports threatened the dominance of even the United States. The strategy that effected this transformation was worked out by private enterprise working in close collaboration with MITI. The main drive of policy was toward innovation — the creation of new industries rather than support for the old. On occasion the government was not loath to assist ailing or sunset industries by relaxing antimonopoly laws, but it did so without impeding the flow of resources to new and profitable sectors. In 1958 Japan made a critical decision to substitute oil for coal. By the first oil shock of 1973, its economy was sufficiently strong to absorb the additional fuel costs without much difficulty. Japan also accepted the decline of its textile and labor-intensive industries. During the 1980s the dangers of environmental pollution and the shortage of sites for heavy industries put a brake on further growth at home of certain industries, such as the primary branches of iron and steel production. At the same time, faced with intense competition from NIC's (newly industrializing countries) such as Taiwan, Singapore and South Korea in large-scale, capital-intensive sectors, Japan has shifted its sights to knowledge-intensive industries — computers, microchips and precision instruments. Japan also avoided the enticements of prestige projects such as the Concorde, which held out little hope of commercial success. Its policy in regard to the aircraft industry was typical. Japan let others do the research and development at vast expense, then bought the finished product when it had reached the marketable stage. The economic strategy was, basically, to select industries carefully, prevent ruinous competition at the infancy stage, nurse them to a competitive stature and then expose them to outside competition. Further, the nursing period was rarely prolonged beyond 10 years. Much of the success of this strategy is associated with the choice of industries and the direction of investment into manufactures for which domestic and world demand is both income-elastic and price-elastic such as for motorcycles, automobiles, steel, electronic apparatuses and shipbuilding. These are industries in which the costs and so prices could be reduced steeply through technological advances and the introduction of mass production methods. Japan gained a large share of world markets in steel, motorcyles, automobiles and electronics by simplifying construction for large economies of scale. Its manufactures also maintain at the same time the highest standards of quality because of its conscientious work force. Foreign observers have been impressed by the fact of the relatively few supervisors and inspectors in Japanese plants.

The devices by which industrial policy is carried out are very comprehensive. The control exercised by the central monetary authorities over bank lending is used to promote high investment in the manufacturing industry, and the rates of interest are held below the natural level and manipulated to that end. Infant industries selected for development are afforded the protection of high tariffs and quantitative import controls. The government provides subsidies to cover the cost of investment in new plants, and firms intent on penetrating foreign markets receive favorable treatment. Export bills are discounted at low rates. The taxation system also plays a significant part in encouraging industrial investment. Securities are exempted from capital gains tax, and depreciation allowances are lavish. Revenues earned from exports are shielded from tax claims by provisions concerning special reserves and accelerated depreciation. Research and development receive special tax concessions. Dumping is encouraged as a means of gaining a foothold in foreign markets. Whereas in many countries government intervention has the effect of protecting the status quo, in Japan it has the opposite effect of encouraging the more enterprising over the more timid, and structural change over laissez-faire.

As in other countries, rapid industrial expansion provides ample opportunities for entrants and so is hostile to concentration. For instance, in 1958, when the automobile industry was still relatively small, there were five manufacturers of passenger cars and nine manufacturers of commercial vehicles. By 1965 the numbers grew to 11 and 13, respectively. Nevertheless, as a result of a consolidation movement in the late 1960s that affected many Japanese industries, concentration increased. This movement was associated in part with the introduction of new technology and in part with the exposure of Japanese industries to increased foreign competition. The early and middle 1960s was a period in which the emphasis was on bigness. Larger units were considered synonymous with efficiency. Hence there was a spate of combinations (*kombinat*). In heavy engineering it led to the rise of Mitsubishi and in automobiles to the rise of Toyota and Nissan. Such combinations, ostensibly in a process by which industries adapted their organization to changes in techniques and demand, were in fact part of an overall strategy by the *keiretsu* to gain advantage over their rivals. In an economy distinguished by constant struggles among oligopolists to increase market shares, concentration was compatible with vigorous competition among the few. The size of the oligopolistic sector is estimated at about 22% of total production. If manufacturing is considered separately, the oligopolistic share is about 35%, with higher-than-average concentrations in automobiles and steel. The concentration rate among the 100 largest firms rose between 1953 and 1964 but declined subsequently as the birth of new firms offset the mergers of the old. With the end of the period of high growth in 1973, concentration again increased in a number of industries. At the same, the growth of megafirms multiplied the opportunities for the smaller and medium-size ones.

Nevertheless, cartels have only marginal influence on market behavior. Historically, the life of a typical Japanese cartel is precarious. Attempts to maintain prices by agreement seldom survive the onset of a recession. Even the iron and steel industry was unable to maintain a cartel because of a large number of fringe producers and fierce competition among them. Restrictive practices were successful only in chemicals, where output and prices were subject to central control. Although established manufacturers and the government were well disposed toward restrictive trade practices, innovative entrepreneurs found little difficulty in breaking through the restraints, and intense rivalries have tempered attempts to create a comfortable regime of oligopolistic stagnation. The dynamism and resilience of Japanse entrepreneurs have always successfully overcome the *zaibatsu* traditions in the economy.

Important elements in Japanese industrial organization are the *sogo shosha* (general trading companies). Fifteen such companies account for 55% of the country's foreign trade. Some of them came into existence as part of the old *zaibatsu*, and Mitsubishi Trading Company and Mitsui Trading Company still are leaders. With branches all over the world and employing over 100,000 people, they are the channels through which technical and marketing developments from abroad reach Japan, and they themselves often take the initiative in introducing new lines of production. These companies' hold over the economy has been strengthened by their association with banks, shipping lines, insurance companies and manufacturing firms.

Japan's endowment as a great industrial nation includes not only the vigor of its industrial organization and the structural adaptability that enables the sector to adapt to new conditions and demands, but also the impressive scientific and technological advances in its laboratories. Annual expenditures on industrial research and development have exceeded 2% since the 1970s and are in the same league as in West Germany and the United States. However, there are significant differences. Some 45% of expenditures in R&D is devoted in the United States and the United Kingdom to defense. Again, in Japan, in contrast to the West, by far the larger part of research initially was in adaptation of superior Western technology rather than in basic research. Now that Japan has achieved parity in technology with the West, more basic research is being undertaken in Japan. Within 25 years Japan has moved from the status of an assimilator to that of an innovator. Its share of foreign patenting in the United States exceeds that of any other foreign country.

The most numerous of the private enterprises on which industrial activity is founded are some 4 million single proprietorships. The dominant form of organization, however, is the corporation, of which there are over 2 million, employing half the labor force. The favored type of organization is the joint stock company, with many features similar to those in the West. They are distinguished from their Western counterparts by their management techniques and market relations.

With the dissolution of the giant *zaibatsu* during the Allied Occupation (1945–52), the corporate system lost the stark dualism that characterized the prewar era and assumed a more graduated structure. The new corporate unit is called the *keiretsu* (linked group or affiliated group). Within the *keiretsu* there are three types of groupings. The first include the heirs of the prewar *zaibatsu*, the second those clustered around a major city bank and the third those clustered around a major industrial producer. Theoretically, a *keiretsu* does not have any central control over its members, and there is no holding company, which still is illegal. The linkage arises from formalized mutual interests, such as swapped directorates and exchange of shares. More importantly, there is a financial nexus through the central institution that provides credit and advice and that also purchases all or most of the output of the smaller satellite companies. The *kinyu keiretsu*, also called *yushi keiretsu* (financially linked group), is only loosely linked, unlike the ex-*zaibatsu* companies. The shares of capital exchanged between a *keiretsu* bank and members do not give any strong controlling interest. A member, however, obtains most of its funds from the bank and receives preferential credit allocation. A member is free to leave without formal permission, in which case it sells the shares it holds in the bank, and the bank sells the shares it holds in the company. Another form of the *kinyu keiretsu* is one in which a trading company performs the role of the bank and in addition sells the products of the members and supplies them with loans. In the case of *sangyo keiretsu*, also called *kigyo keiretsu*, the central company has a substantial degree of control over its industrially linked satellites and is the main or the only buyer of their products. Some of the central companies of a *sangyo keiretsu* may themselves belong to a *kinyu keiretsu*; for example, Toshiba and Toyota belong to the Mitsui *kinyu keiretsu*. None of these various *keiretsu* is a monopoly. They represent neither vertical nor horizontal integration. The financial bonds among members of the group vary. The bank's shareholdings of any company cannot by law exceed 10% and, in fact, they are well below the maximum limit. However, the share of the loans provided by a bank often goes up to 50% or 60%, giving it effective control over company management. A further link is provided by exchanged directorates. Coordination takes place at periodic meetings of corporation executives. The purpose of these meetings is to exchange information and ideas rather than to lay down directives.

Relationships are slightly different in the *sangyo keiretsu*, where members of the group are often subsidiaries, subcontractors or affiliates of the parent firm. The larger firm concentrates on final assembly and high value-added processes, while the smaller ones perform specialized and labor-intensive tasks. Cash payments to the subcontractors are supplemented by commercial bills whose maturity could be postponed when the need arose. Subcontractors account for 60% of Japan's 6 million small and medium-size enterprises. For example, Toyota has over 40,000 subcontractors who furnish 60% of parts, helping Toyota to maintain low inventories.

While theoretically the corporations are owned by the stockholders, the rate of individual ownership is falling and now is less than 30%. Financial corporations account for the remaining 70%. Relative to capital, almost all large Japanese corporations carry enormous debt, a phenomenon known as overborrowing. Such an unbalanced capital structure results from the easy availability of credit from the main group bank and the network of corporate relations, which reduces the need to resort to capital markets. Corporate shareholder meetings are often only window dressing. Some companies even hire thugs to terrorize stockholders into voting as management desires. The auditing system is also poorly developed. Until recently few companies engaged outside auditors, and accounting practices give corporations leeway to mislead both the public and the stockholders. To control this type of excess, the law was changed in 1981 to enhance the power of auditors and to reduce the number of stockholders in the employ of management. In general, managements do much as they please, with little public accountability.

The Japanese style of management has gained considerable attention in recent years because it is regarded as one of the principal ingredients of Japan's industrial success. The organization of management itself presents some peculiar features. Foreigners always have had difficulty in identifying the sources of authority in any organization because they expect to find responsibilities clearly assigned to individuals. But the significant management unit in Japan is not an individual manager but a cluster of people with joint responsibilities. At every level the units have their spokesmen or representatives, who report to the next-highest group in the hierarchy. Thus individual responsibility is vaguely defined, and it is difficult to tell where management begins or ends. To the Japanese a precise definition of responsibilities seems otiose, since every person is first and foremost a member of a team, which identifies itself unreservedly with the firm's interests. Thus there are no bosses in Japan but only boss groups. Dominating personalities assert themselves by becoming the nuclei around which managerial personnel at various levels cluster. Thus coteries and cliques are familiar features of the business landscape. Although hierarchically structured, decision-making is not a one-way, top-to-bottom process. All decisions involve *ring-sei*, a two-way flow of information to which all members of a group have input. Although *ring-sei* is time-consuming and often a convenient way of avoiding responsibility, it works well in practice. Because of the wider diffusion of responsibility and the involvement of everyone concerned, execution is rapid and efficient once a decision is made.

The system also stresses strong company loyalty. The Japanese have no use for the inspired lone ranger or prima donna. As a result, the Japanese worker tends to be emotionally involved in the fortunes of the company in a way seldom found in other countries. They are, indeed, so completely devoted to the business they serve as to leave little room for private social activities other than those with their fellow workers. Once recruited by a firm, they are expected to remain with it for the rest of their working life, although some may move to affiliated companies within the same group.

The basic unit of corporate organization is the section, consisting normally of about 20 workers at the lowest level. Several sections form the next highest level, the department, a number of which, in the larger corporations, form a division. The section chief leads his group as a team leader and, ideally, as a father figure. Subordinates rarely call him by name but always address him as "Mr. Section Chief." Section chiefs often are generalists who understand company operations through long years of service. Most sections are devoid of physical barriers such as private office space. To reinforce the sense of group cohesiveness, the section chief frequently entertains his staff at drinking or eating establishments and participates in their major family occasions.

The main decision-making body is the executive committee, consisting of all directors above the rank of managing director. Managing directors are responsible for functional areas of corporate activity and are assisted by junior directors.

Although the overriding corporate goal is the maximization of profits and sales, prestige plays a prominent role in the corporate ethos, as is to be expected in a society where "face" and "shame" are guiding social determinants. Maintaining high dividends receives a low priority, and shareholders in general receive little attention.

The management system is not static and is slowly changing in response to internal social dynamics as well as the influence of American styles. Seniority-based promotions are being questioned, and corporate headhunting is becoming popular. However, the hold of tradition still is strong, given its successful mission of transforming Japan into an industrial giant.

The geographical distribution of industry is skewed, first, in favor of the coastal areas, and second, within these coastal areas, in favor of two zones, one between Tokyo Bay and Osaka Bay and between Osaka and the Strait of Shimonoseki. The 1,006 km. (625 mi.) from the capital to Nagasaki contain about 85% of all manufacturing plants. The width of the belt varies, becoming broader in the plains of Kanto, Nagoya and Osaka, and occasionally contracting until it disappears completely in the areas between Atami and Numazu in several places on the Inland Sea. Tokyo itself furnishes one-third of all manufacturing capacity and Osaka one-fourth. Such heavy concentration has been viewed disfavorably by economic planners, who are encouraging the spread of industry along the Pacific coast north of the capital.

Japan's iron and steel production is the largest in the non-Communist world, having surpassed that of the United States in the 1970s. Three-quarters of the production is controlled by five major firms. The country has been a world leader in adopting two important innovations in steel-making: basic oxygen furnaces and the continuous casting process. The industry also has been converting from petroleum sources of energy to coal. The industry, however, is characterized by high fixed costs and unstable demand. The steel firms, moreover, tend to be undiversified and thus are vulnerable to slumps and recessions. In the nonferrous metal industry, copper, lead and zinc smelting and the production of wires and cables survived the second energy crisis, but the aluminum industry collapsed. The petrochemicals industry is the world's second-largest but is increasingly dependent on overseas projects and new innovative processes. Future growth depends on breakthroughs in biotechnology.

Japan is the world's largest producer of motor vehicles. It also is the world's largest exporter of motor vehicles and motorcycles. The rise of Japanese automobiles as a factor in international markets has been meteoric. In the 1950s Japan hardly had any auto industry; by 1965 it exported only 200,000 units. By 1980 production had exceeded 11.04 million units (thus surpassing the United States) and exports 6.12 million units. Production soared still further, to 12 million units by the mid-1980s. The automobile industry is dominated by nine companies: Toyota, the leader; Nissan (Datsun); Toyo Kogyo (Mazda); Mitsubishi; Honda; Isuzu; Fuji (Subaru); Suzuki; and Haihatsu. Foreign ownership in the industry includes 25% of Toyo Kogyo by Ford, 34% of Isuzu by General Motors and 15% of Mitsubishi by Chrysler. Japan's auto industry is more independent of government assistance than is typical of other industries. This is particularly true of mavericks such as Honda. Japanese contribution to automobile technology has been mainly in miniaturization; process technology; and development of new engines, such as Honda's CVCC and Mazda's rotary.

Japan dominates world shipbuilding, with more than half of all orders. Its closest competitors are South Korea and Spain, with 9% and 5.2%, respectively. Japan's rise in shipbuilding has displaced the European countries which, until the 1970s, were leaders. Japanese shipyards are able to outperform European ones through advanced design, fast delivery and low costs of production. Production methods are among the most innovative and include new welding techniques and a process called zone outfitting in which ship units are fabricated on land.

The fourth area of Japanese industrial leadership is electronics, including radios and television sets, in which Japanese have managed to eliminate the competition in most countries of the world. In electronics as in other products, the Japanese are shifting production to foreign countries. In video recorders the Japanese share is virtually total.

Japan was a latecomer to the computer industry, but by 1980 it was second only to the United States. Fujitsu, the largest domestic firm, surpassed IBM in 1979 as a supplier of the Japanese market. By 1980 the technologies of large and small computers had caught up with those in the United States. However, Japanese software still lags. The most spectacular computer success has been in the design and manufacture of semiconductors, of which Japan was a net importer until 1977. By 1977 Japan had caught up with the United States in many facets of semiconductor technology, and in certain areas, such as in the production of 16K RAM (random-access memory), gained the lead.

The fifth area of industrial leadership is machine tools and robotics, which is the third-largest in the non-Communist world, after the United States and West Germany. Machine tools are highly specialized in function and are made by relatively small firms. Japan is the world leader in robot application focused on simple, small-scale and low-cost machines that can be programmed for short production runs. Robots are expected to enhance the capability of Japanese industries to compete in world markets.

MANUFACTURING INDICATORS, 1986

Average annual growth rate 1980–86: 7.8%

Share of GDP: 30% (1986)

Labor force in manufacturing: 34.1

Value added in manufacturing, 1985: $395.148 billion
  Food & agriculture: 10%
  Textiles: 6%
  Machinery: 37%
  Chemicals: 9%

Earnings per employee in manufacturing:
  Growth Rate Index (1980=100): (1980-85) 113 (1985)

Total Earnings as % of value added: 36

Gross output per employee (1980=100): 130 (1986)

Index of Manufacturing Production (1980=100): 134 (1988)

MINING

Japan's only mineral resource is coal. Domestic production declined from a peak of 55 million tons in 1960 to 16.382 million tons in 1985, which meets only 15% of the total domestic consumption of 109 million tons. Hampered by high production costs and competition from cheap supplies of foreign coal, the major coal companies are operating at a chronic deficit. Employment in mining attracts fewer workers. Further, the nation's 1 million tons of reserves are almost all hard coal used for coking. Most of the coal is converted into electric power.

Japanese coal is of recent origin and is found for the most part in opposite ends of the country, in Hokkaido and Kyushu, which possess 45% and 40%, respectively, of all coal deposits. The coal deposits of Kyushu are of poor quality and difficult to extract, but the proximity of the mines to the sea facilitates transportation. In Hokkaido the seams are wider and therefore can be worked mechanically, and the quality is good. However, the mines are distant from the sea. In most mines, inclined galleries are used instead of pits, extending in places as much as 9.7 km. (6 mi.) underground. This is a costly procedure despite the installation of moving platforms. A miner's daily output is therefore far less than that in Europe and the United States. In these circumstances, domestic coal costs more than imported coal.

ENERGY

Since 1945 the rapid development of industry has doubled the demand for power about once every five years. The use of power also has changed qualitatively. In 1950 coal supplied half the needs of the country, hydroelectricity one-third and oil the rest. Between 1960 and 1972, a period of accelerated growth, energy demand persistently outstripped increments of the GNP, with the result that Japan's share of world energy doubled. In 1976, with oil supplying 74% of primary energy, the Japanese demand for oil exceeded that of Africa, China, India, Pakistan and Eastern Europe combined. With only 3% of the world's population, Japan was consuming 6% of the global energy supplies.

No country in the world is more dependent than Japan on fuel imports. Almost 90% of the country's energy is hauled from the outside. An embargo on foreign oil supplies would paralyze the economy within a few months. Japan has virtually no oil production, and the emphasis is on shipment from producing countries, refining and marketing. Even in the case of refining and marketing companies, ownership is shared with foreign interests such as Caltex, Exxon, Shell, Mobil and others. Idemitsu is the only Japanese company free of foreign interests. There is no vertical system from wellhead to consumer, as in the United States. Since 1973 dependence has been shifting from the international cartels to Arab and Iranian producers, giving Japan more flexibility in negotiating advantageous business deals regarding supply and prices. Energy policy has a twofold objective: (1) to secure new sources of supply outside the Middle East (e.g., from China, the Soviet Union and Malaysia) through offer of large-scale investments; and (2) to court the Arab states and Iran through political support. At present Japan has a 84-day stockpile stored in giant storage tanks, including the world's largest, at Kiire.

Conservation measures have been more effective in industry than in the private sector. There has been little effort to promote district heating and insulation. The major industrial energy consumers reduced their dependence on oil by 23% between 1973 and 1980, while the overall consumption of energy per unit of output fell by 14% during that period. At the same time, the power industry reduced its dependence on oil by 16%. By 1990 the overall dependence on oil is expected to fall to about 47% of all energy.

Japan is the third largest producer of electricity in the world. The majority of the over 3,300 plants are thermoelectric. Three-quarters of the available power is controlled by the 10 major regional power utilities, of which Tokyo Electric Power Company is the largest in the world. Japanese electricity rates are among the highest in the world.

Since the 1980s nuclear power has become increasingly prominent in the energy budget. Although a late starter, Japan borrowed technology from the United States and contracted for uranium from Canada, France, South Africa and Australia. By 1987 there were 36 nuclear reactors in operation, with three additional reactors planned or under construction. Since 1980 the program has encountered severe opposition from environmental groups, particularly following the Three-Mile Island accident in the United States. There were other setbacks and obstacles, including the rising prices of nuclear reactors and fuel; the huge investments required for fuel enrichment and reprocessing plants; reactor failures; the problem of nuclear waste disposal; and most importantly, the Chernobyl disaster. For meteorological reasons, heat from nuclear plants cannot be discharged from cooling towers but requires a large amount of warm water, which creates thermal pollution on a grand scale.

Whereas the nuclear industry is closely controlled by the government in most other countries, it has been in private hands in Japan from the very beginning. The government provides research assistance through the Japan Atomic Energy Research Institute, the Power Reactors and Nuclear Fuel Development Corporation, the Atomic Energy Bureau and the Japan Atomic Industrial Forum. The Japan Atomic Energy Commission is the principal policy forum, while safety matters are monitored by Nuclear Safety Bureau and the Japan Nuclear Safety Commission.

Of the other alternate sources of energy, Japan has effectively exploited only geothermal energy. Japan has at present six geothermal power stations with a combined capacity of 133,000 kw.-hr.

ENERGY INDICATORS, 1986

Primary Energy Production (quadrillion Btu)
    Crude oil: 0.03
    Natural gas liquid: —
    Dry natural gas: 0.10
    Coal: 0.39
    Hydroelectric power: 0.81
    Nuclear power: 1.67
    Total: 2.99
Average annual energy production growth rate (1980–86):
    5.3%
Public utilities' share of GDP: 3%
Energy consumption per capita (kg. oil equivalent): 3,186
Energy imports as % of merchandise imports: 18
Average annual growth rate of energy consumption
    (1980–86): 1.5%

Electricity
    Installed capacity: 169,528,000 kw.
    Production: 673.412 billion kw-hr.
      % fossil fuel: 63
      % hydro: 13.1
      % nuclear: 23.7
    Consumption per capita: 5,577

Natural gas
    Proved reserves: 32 billion cubic m
    Production: 2.291 million tons
    Consumption: 38.079 million tons

Petroleum
    Proved reserves: 58 million barrels
    Years to exhaust proved reserves: 15
    Production: 4 million barrels
    Consumption: 1.611 billion barrels
    Refining capacity: 4.790 million barrels per day

Coal
    Reserves: 1.015 billion tons
    Production: 16.382 million tons
    Consumption: 109.46 million tons

LABOR

The Japanese labor force is estimated at 59.6 million, representing a participation rate of 68%. The sectoral distribution is 11% in agriculture, 34% in industry and 55% in services. Compared to other industrial countries, the percentage in agriculture is higher and that in services is lower. The services sector is not as highly developed because a large percentage of the work force is in the export-oriented manufacturing sector and the protected agricultural sector. According to a study by the Ministry of Labor, the share of services will rise to 60% by 1990.

The workplace still is governed by basic labor laws passed under the Allied Occupation. These include the Labor Standards Law of 1947 and the Trade Union Law and the Labor Relations Adjustment Act of 1946. The latter two give workers the right to bargain collectively and to strike, and govern the machinery for arbitration and mediation and for the public regulation of wages. Almost identical with the U.S. Wagner Act, they contain a set of prohibitions against unfair labor practices. The Labor Standards Law embodies the standards and recommendations of the ILO.

One of the most widely publicized features of the Japanese labor market is what has been called "permanent commitment." This often is interpreted to mean that once a blue-collar or a white-collar employee achieves a regular status with a firm, he is guaranteed employment with the same firm for the duration of his career, regardless of his performance or the firm's need for his services. The system, however, is not that simple. Ideally an employee is hired directly from school or college and, after a probationary period, achieves a tenured status under which he can be discharged only for specified reasons, such as lengthy, unexcused absenteeism; behavior detrimental to the company's reputation; involvement in fights; or commission of crimes, all of which are very rare. The employee is not subject to discharge or even to temporary layoff, either because a decline in business renders his services superfluous to the firm or because his services are not up to par. He may, of course, resign, but this also is unusual. Tenure continues to age 55, when retirement is compulsory. The system is not a holdover from feudal times but is of comparatively recent origin, after World War II. Although practiced formally by a majority of firms, the custom is not universal. Female employees are generally excluded from the system because of frequent breaks in their working life as a result of marriage and pregnancy. There are departures from the ideal lifetime permanent employment pattern for males as well. A good many young men leave their jobs voluntarily because the work is too demanding or monotonous or both. Troublesome employees are eased out or induced to resign. One consequence of the system is the reluctance of corporations to hire midcareer or older workers, to poach another firm for employees or to hire its former employees. The system ensures that Japan has a very low turnover rate. In the 20- to 24-year category for males, the turnover rate is one-fourth that in the United States.

The permanent commitment does not imply that Japanese firms are unable to adjust their personnel strength during periods of economic fluctuation. One means is to cut overtime, bonuses and allowances. Another is to discharge part-time workers and dispense with the employees of subcontractors. Thus these two categories of employees are used to cushion the shocks of fluctuations in demand and enable the corporations to maintain some flexibility in their payroll staff. Another cost-reducing element is the retirement system. Most retirees continue to work beyond the mandatory retirement age, although at reduced salaries, usually in subsidiaries or subcontractors of their original employers. They constitute a reservoir of relatively cheap labor prepared to accept short-term employment. Permanent commitment, far from being a burden on management, offers it a number of compensating benefits. One is that it reduces union militancy. Employees enjoying security of job need less recourse to unions. Second, employers have a virtually free hand in allocating labor across geographical, craft and industrial boundaries. Third, it helps build company loyalty and morale and thus is a potent source for higher productivity.

A second characteristic of the labor market is *nenko*, or the seniority wage system in which earnings are related solely to length of service regardless of skill, past experience, position or degree of responsibility. Under *nenko*, age is the basic factor in determining the standard wage profile, but accumulated merit credits for length of service can be a crucial determinant in the order of promotions between two persons with otherwise equal qualifications. Pure *nenko* is observed only in government offices, but even here separate elite tracks and accelerated promotion dilute the system somewhat. *Nenko* is extremely egalitarian in character and works best in a homogeneous society where all workers have more or less equal working ability and other endowments. The system is not well suited to deal with inferior and inefficient members of an organization. As a result, more job-oriented wage systems are being implemented by management. Usually they are called job ability payment (*shokuno-kyu*) programs. Some elements of *nenko* are not eliminated from the new programs, which integrate both principles: remuneration according to age and remuneration according to ability. *Nenko* has functioned smoothly in a surplus labor market in which highly motivated workers could be recruited with ease and were content with meager starting salaries because *nenko* guaranteed a rising income in the future. But with the aging of the labor force combined with labor shortages, *nenko* is being increasingly replaced with performance-linked programs.

According to the government's White Paper on Women Workers for 1986, the number of women employees reached 23.95 million. In 1985, for the first time, the number of working women exceeded the number of full-time housewives. The number of female workers has tripled since 1955, while the number of male workers has grown more slowly, by 2.2 times. In 1986 a total of 40% of all employees were women. However, traditional attitudes have not disappeared completely from the workplace. Compensation for women, including bonuses, is only 52% of that for men. A large and rising proportion of new temporary and part-time workers are women (22.1% in 1984, up from 17.4% in 1975). The reason is that women continue to drop temporarily out of the labor force during their 20s and 30s (the so-called M-shaped female participation curve). In doing so they are themselves dropped by the system. In some firms women are expected to retire upon marriage.

In 1985, the final year of the U.N. Decade for Women, the Japanese government ratified the U.N. Convention on the Elimination of All Forms of Discrimination Against Women after enacting the Equal Employment Opportunity Law, which went into effect in April 1986. Under the law, employers are required to extend equal treatment to men and women in job offers, recruitment, assignment and promotion and not to discriminate against women regarding training, welfare benefits and retirement age. Disputes are mediated by the Equal Opportunity Commission.

Another facet of the labor scene is the emphasis on productivity, which has attained the status of a business creed. The productivity movement began in 1955 as an alliance of businessmen, trade unionists and academics seeking to find a way to bring industrial peace to Japan. Contrary to current popular belief, Japanese industrial relations have not always been harmonious. From the immediate postwar period until the early 1960s the country was racked by large-scale industrial unrest. As the productivity movement gained strength, the unrest subsided, most dramatically in the private sector. Productivity is partially linked to strict quality control based on such practices as quality control circles, where workers actively participate in eliminating product defects and share decision-making with management. There is close cooperation among members of a work team. Work targets and methods are agreed on by all members of a work unit. Managers and executives do not isolate themselves from workers and often work on the shop floor, doing menial and routine jobs along with blue-collar workers.

Japan does not have a universal minimum wage. Rather, a law adopted in 1959 provides for the Ministry of Labor to set minimum wages by industry, occupation or region. Recommendations are made by tripartite councils established at the central and prefectural levels. To ensure the coherent administration of the law, the Central Minimum Wages Council reviews the activities of the prefectural councils and provides guidance. The prefectures are divided into four "ranks," each of which has its own standard for setting minimum wages.

The minimum wage is revised annually, and the general prefectural minimum wage is normally lower than the industrial one. There are significant differences between the highest rate, which regularly applies to Tokyo and Osaka, and the lowest (e.g., in Okinawa).

Wage demands are put forward by national unions in an annual rite known as *shunto* (spring offensive). Although the claims are pressed by all unions, the unions in the major industries take the lead in the offensive. The employers derive certain advantages from such a concerted offensive, as it eliminates piecemeal claims and settlements known as "leapfrogging."

Wages vary by industry and employment. For regular workers in firms with more than 30 employees, those in finance, real estate, public service, iron and steel, petroleum and publishing earn the highest wages. The lowest-paid are those in textiles, apparel, furniture and the leather products industries. The receipts of the average farmer are even lower. The salaries of administrative and technical workers are about 20% higher than those of production workers. Wages vary according to size of enterprise as well. With wages in manufacturing firms having 500 employees or more indexed at 100, enterprises with 100 to 499 employees are indexed at 79, those with 30 to 99 employees at 64 and those with five to 29 employees at 56.6. The gap between wages paid to high-school graduates and to university graduates is slight at entry level but widens with age and peaks at 55, when the former receive only 60% to 80% of the wages of the latter. Wage differentials are relatively small between blue-collar workers and administrative personnel and between administrative personnel and management executives. On the whole, the real earnings of Japanese workers have risen faster than those in the West since 1960.

In addition to regular monthly contract earnings, Japanese employees receive fairly large bonuses, both at the middle and at the end of each calendar year. The system of bonuses is important in two ways. First, it provides the employer with a means of reducing labor costs during recessions by adjusting the amount of bonus, although this is not determined unilaterally but is subject to collective bargaining. Generally it is equal to two to three months' wages. Second, bonuses influence the spending pattern of workers and boost July and December purchases of durable goods. In addition to bonuses, Japanese workers receive a number of fringe benefits, such as living allowances, incentive payments, remuneration for special job conditions, allowances for good attendance and cost-of-living allowances. Employees also receive three major nonwage benefits: severance pay; various payments in kind; and welfare, recreational, housing and vacation benefits.

The legal workweek is eight hours a day, not to exceed 48 hours a week. The overtime premium for work in excess of 48 hours is at least 25%. Of all the major industrial democracies, Japan has the longest hours of actual work—slightly over 2,100 hours per year. Repeated efforts by unions to have the workweek reduced legislatively to the international norm of 40 hours have so far failed. One novel and controversial feature of worktime is the prevalence of voluntary, uncompensated overtime performed particularly in the white-collar field, including the regular feature of employees taking no more than 60% of their legally due vacations. This phenomenon is related to the internal dynamics of the work team *(ka)* under which no individual will take time off unless everyone else in the *ka* is doing so. It also may be due to a genuine preference by male workers for the camaraderie of the workplace to the cramped accommodations of the typical Japanese home.

The unemployment rate in December 1987 was 2.6%, down from 3.1% in May 1987. Although overall unemployment has fallen rapidly, labor market mismatches have tended to worsen, with increased unemployment in rural areas and in those areas heavily dependent on manufacturing sectors hard hit by the stronger yen. While the labor force rose by 1% in 1987, the decline in labor force participation rates continued for both males and females.

Established in 1947, the unemployment insurance system is overseen by the Ministry of Labor but administered, for the most part, by local authorities. The system covers almost all employees other than seasonal workers, seamen and government employees. Coverage, however, is voluntary for employees in firms with under five workers. Benefits are keyed to a percentage of the previous earnings (up to 80% for low-wage earners), and their duration is based on an individual's age, the existence of a handicap and whether an individual was insured for less or more than one year. Additional benefits are available for training and job searches.

The enterprise union system is described as one of the three "precious treasures of industrial relations," the other two being *nenko* and lifetime employment. Enterprise unions are autonomous worker organizations representing only all regular employees of a given enterprise. The Japanese like to contrast this system, with its single focus on an individual enterprise, with those in other countries in which workers are organized in multiemployer unions based on an industry or a craft. Although enterprise unions federate themselves into industrial and national structures, they retain their autonomy, and their ambit is limited to the home base firm. Almost all Japanese trade unions are enterprise unions (the only notable exception being the Seamen's Union), and in the largest firms there normally is only one such union. In the case of multiplant firms, separate unions are commonly formed for each plant, and these are linked together in the organization that covers all the firm's workers, irrespective of the industry in which the members are engaged. This explains the large number of trade unions in Japan, over 74,499 of them, of which 94% are enterprise unions.

The ratio of union members to total employment is less than 29%, much lower than it was 10 years ago. About 28% are women, and a high proportion are white-collar workers. The organization rate varies from industry to industry and also according to the size of the enterprise. The most completely organized industries are public utilities and government service, with transportation and public communications close behind. One peculiarity is the strength of unionization among white-collar workers, who are among the most militant. Almost one-quarter of the union members—35% if government service and services are included—are white-collar workers. The phenomenon of a common organization for blue- and white-collar workers, rare in the West, has helped to inhibit the emergence of class distinctions in the workplace. In large firms, all but the most senior-level management officials were union officials at one stage in their careers, and it is not unusual for a personnel manager to have been a union official once. In the private sector, unionism is confined primarily to the larger companies.

The national unions are, with a few notable exceptions, loose associations of enterprise local unions without either legal or customary authority over their policies. Most national union leaders owe their power to their base enterprise union rather than the national unions. Many national unions also suffer from the failure of many enterprise unions to affiliate with them.

Japan's over 74,499 trade unions are clustered around four "national centers":

Sohyo (the General Council of the Trade Unions of Japan), established in 1950, is the largest of the centers, with 4.36 million members. Sohyo is largely a federation of public sector unions, including the two largest: Jichiro, of local government employees, and Nikkyoso, of teachers. Politically it is an active supporter of the Japan Socialist Party but is not affiliated with any international federation.

Domei (the Japanese Confederation of Labor), established in 1964 by moderate unions unhappy with Sohyo, is the latter's main rival. Almost exclusively a private-sector organization, with 2.16 million members, its strength lies in middle-size firms. Politically it supports the Democratic Socialist Party and is affiliated with the International Confederation of Free Trade Unions.

Churitsuroren (the Federation of Independent Unions of Japan), founded in 1956, has the strongest national headquarters structure. With 1.56 million members it is the third-largest of the centers and has only private-sector affiliates. Politically it supports the Japan Socialist Party but is unaffiliated to any international organization.

Shinsanbetsu (the National Federation of Industrial Organizations) is the smallest of the centers, with only 61,000 members.

Current efforts to unify the labor movement are based on the 1982 creation by private-sector unions of Zenkin Rokyo (the Japanese Private-Sector Trade Union Council). Zenkin Rokyo has 60 member unions representing 5.3 million private-sector workers. One of the main objectives of unifying the unions is to increase organized labor's political influence. Another is to find a way to deal with the relative stagnation, in absolute terms, of union membership, which now is less than 29%. Despite this stagnation, most unions, thanks to their high dues structures, are relatively affluent and are able to maintain large staffs, conduct wide-ranging international activities and accumulate substantial strike funds. However, the bulk of union assets are retained by the local unions.

Large enterprise unions have full-time officers and small ones part-time officers. But virtually all small unions and some large ones are given office space by the employer and use company facilities for membership meetings. Litigation is the exception rather than the rule. The lack of a cadre of professional officers at the local level is regarded as a major source of weakness in the labor movement. Worker representatives who retain their status as company employees are not in a position to resist management pressures. Further, unions are run by the company's key employees, usually first- and second-line supervisors, whose career interests and advancement lie in the promotion of, not in opposition to, management interests.

The most representative organization of employers is Nikkeiren (the Japan Federation of Employer Associations), with a membership of some 31,000 corporations. It is organized into three regional associations and 55 industrial associations. It engages in policy studies, makes recommendations, liaises with government and unions, offers training programs and conducts research but does not engage in collective bargaining. It maintains close contacts with Keidanren (the Federation of Economic Organizations), which represents major coporations on matters other than labor and social issues.

On an average, Japan loses the fewest worker-days to industrial disputes of any of the industrial democracies. In 1984 a total of 4,480 industrial disputes were reported, involving 3,652,000 workers. Of these only 594 lasted more than one day. Since 1981 the average number of days lost per worker per year to disputes was 0.011, contrasted with 0.129 in the United States. The largest number of disputes in Japan occur in the public and services sector, and the largest number of days lost are in manufacturing, communications and transportation.

Japanese industrial relations law, in general, dates from the Occupation period and has certain features that reflect American inspiration. Under Articles 12 and 28 of the Constitution, all citizens have an "eternal and inalienable right" to "organize and act" collectively. The scope of these constitutional guarantees goes beyond those in many countries, and the right to act, in particular, has been interpreted by the courts as extending considerably beyond just the right to organize, to bargain collectively and to strike.

The Trade Union Law, which covers almost all nonpublic employees, implements those rights and proscribes an employer's refusal to bargain collectively as an "unfair (or improper) labor practice." To adjudicate complaints of unfair labor practices, a system of tripartite prefectural labor relations commissions exists, together with an appellate Central Labor Relations Commission in Tokyo. (There is a separate system and commission for the maritime industry.) The authority of the commissions extends to all labor disputes, and they are mandated to adjudicate them by "mediation, conciliation and arbitration." However, labor disputes, other than unfair practices complaints, also may be appealed to the courts, which may issue a provisional order or injunction pending final disposition of the complaint.

In its application, Japan labor law is complex, particularly as it relates to unfair labor practices. The unions' exercise of their constitutional rights takes precedence over other legal considerations, and unions and union members are exempt from civil and criminal liability for strikes or "justifiable acts of dispute."

Since 1947 the national civil service and since 1948 all other public employees have been covered by separate statutes. Under these statutes, police, fire fighters, prison employees, the self-defense forces and the coast guard may not form unions, but all other public employees are free to do so. However, the laws prohibit strikes; limit the scope of bargaining; and with the exception of the civil service, provide for various commissions, analogous to those in the private sector, to handle unfair labor practice disputes. The most important of these, the Public Corporation and National Enterprise Labor Relations Commission (KOROI), is tripartite. The Supreme Court has held that prohibition of strikes in the public sector is constitutional because the law, at the same time, provides alternative means of protecting worker interests.

In the private sector it is customary for collective bargaining to cover almost every conceivable aspect of labor-management relations. The results are formalized in what are known as "comprehensive labor agreements." However, issues affecting management and production (new plant and equipment, subcontracting, etc.) normally are handled in regular close consultations between unions and managements rather than made a subject of bargaining.

Curiously, these "comprehensive agreements" normally do not cover wages, which are dealt with in separate annual negotiations held during the *shunto*. These "spring offensives," highly ritualized affairs accompanied by banners, sloganeering and dancing, are intended more as shows of force than as crippling actions. Behind closed doors at the same time, serious discussions take place between managers and union officials over the actual extent of pay raises. Nearly 70% of all workers are affected by the *shunto*. Negotiations are conducted either on a group basis or on an industry basis and take place serially by custom from March through May. The process has given rise to special *shunto*-related special organizational alliances of industrial unions affiliated with different national centers.

In the early years of the *shunto*, when the economy was growing rapidly, there was a labor shortage, and firms were competing for new employees by bidding up wages. This tended to make for rather high *shunto* settlements. In recent years, however, wage gains have been held well below the inflation rate.

LABOR INDICATORS, 1986

Total economically active population: 59.6 million
As % of working-age population: 68
% female: 40 (1986)
Activity rate
    Total: 49.4
    Male: 60.5
    Female: 38.6

Employment status (%)
    Employers & self-employed: 15.4
    Employees: 72.3
    Unpaid family workers: 9.4
    Other: 2.9

Organized labor: 29%

Sectoral employment (%)
    Agriculture, forestry, fishing: 8.8
    Mining: 0.2
    Manufacturing, construction: 34.1
    Electricity, gas, water: 0.6
    Trade: 22.7
    Transportation, communications: 5.9
    Finance, real estate: 6.8
    Services: 21.0

Average annual growth rate of labor force, 1980–2000:
    0.5

Unemployment (%): 2.6 (1987)
Labor under 20 years: 2.7

Hours of work
    Manufacturing: 41.6 per week

In the public sector both wages and conditions of employment are determined by law. The National Personnel Authority (NPA) makes annual recommendations on salary increases for civil servants to the cabinet and the Diet based on the results of wage surveys. In public enterprises, the right to negotiate and conclude agreements exists, but only where related to conditions of employment.

FOREIGN TRADE

International trade is the lifeblood of the Japanese economy. In a purely physical sense, Japan's dependence on trade is an effort to compensate for its paucity of natural resources, including such vital ones as food and fuel. It also reflects Japan's historic tendency in relations with foreign countries to concentrate on areas in which it can gain a dominating position. In any case, Japan in 1987 was the third-greatest trading nation in the world, its trade surpluses surpassing those of West Germany, the United Kingdom and United States, all of whom have longer histories as trading nations. Among non-Communist countries Japan accounts for 10% of the trade of industrialized nations and 7% of all trade. It is the world's largest buyer of raw materials and a major supplier of industrial products and consumer durables. As a prcentage of the GNP, however, Japan exports less than other major trading countries of the world. In 1986 Japan exported 10% of its GNP, compared with 18% for Australia, 20% for France, 23% for Italy, 28% for West Germany and the United Kingdom, 30% for Canada and 57% for the Netherlands. Among industrial democracies only the United States has a lower share of exports in the GNP. Although the Japanese economy is less dependent on foreign markets on the basis of this yardstick, international export markets are extremely important for specific industries. Exports account for half the total production of automobiles, machine tools and television sets and for three-fourths of the production of watches and cameras. In these industries, export markets allow firms to achieve volume sales and economies of large-scale production and to mitigate demand fluctuations. The dependence on foreign trade is a result also of the critical lack of food and raw materials necessary for national survival. Japan is one of the poorest nations in the world in terms of self-sufficiency in natural resources. The Japanese are constantly weighed down by a sense of economic insecurity, heightened by events such as the oil crises of 1973 and 1979 and the U.S. embargo on soybean exports in 1973.

Success in foreign trade has brought Japan worldwide recognition. The label "Made in Japan" no longer carries the stigma of shoddy worksmanship. Once largely dependent on imports of technology, Japan now is also a major exporter of advanced technology and a source of innovation. Once a recipient of aid, Japan is now a donor, although not a very generous one. The Japanese yen, once a currency little traded outside of Japan, now is the hottest monetary unit in capital markets around the globe.

Japan's dominance in foreign trade is of very recent origin. It was only in 1960 that exports reached prewar levels. During the 1960s the dollar value of exports grew at an average annual rate of 16.9%, more than 75% faster than the average rates of all non-communist countries. During the 1970s the growth rate in the domestic economy dropped in half from the double-digit rates of previous decades. This caused industries to look abroad for new markets. Japan also faced sharply higher bills for imported energy and raw materials. As a result, exports continued to grow, at an average annual rate of 21%. Trade grew so rapidly that the United States' trade lead over Japan was whittled down by 60% between 1960 and 1980. During the 1970s, export expansion provided a stimulus to the sluggish domestic economy. In that sense, Japan's recent economic growth has been export-driven, in contrast to the immediate postwar period, when growth in international trade was the result, not the cause, of rapid domestic growth.

Structural changes accompanied growth. In the 1950s two-thirds of the exports went to underdeveloped countries, and developed countries took in less than a third. The development of trade in this period presented something of a paradox. The fastest-growing exports initially were products of capital-intensive industries, because it was in these industries that costs were falling most rapidly in consequence of technical advances. In the developing countries Japan became the preferred supplier for such goods because it was able to compete successfully with European and American products, whereas it had to compete with local manufacturers for labor-intensive goods. On the other hand, Japan's best markets for labor-intensive goods were the richer countries, whose incomes were rising steeply and whose labor costs were higher. By the 1960s Japan's exports to all countries consisted entirely of large-scale capital-intensive industry products. Changes in sources of supply naturally accompanied those in the composition of imports. Japan began to obtain from North America raw materials and food, which previously came from the Third World. What was most galling to the United States was that since the 1970s it has, in relation to Japan, assumed the role of a primary commodity exporter, a role normally assigned to developing economies. The third phase of Japan's foreign trade history began in the 1980s, when rising labor costs relative to the newly industrializing countries (NIC) made its products less competitive in international markets. This has required Japan to move up the technological ladder to more sophisticated and technology-intensive products. Thus within a space of

35 years Japan has moved from textiles, tea and toys to television sets, ships, steel, cameras and cars and finally to computers, copiers and machine tools.

The primary responsibility for formulating and implementing international trade policy rests with the Ministry of International Trade and Industry (MITI). MITI is responsible not only for exports and imports but also for all domestic industries and businesses not specifically covered by other ministries, investments in plants and equipment, pollution control, energy and power, some aspects of foreign economic assistance and consumer complaints. MITI is an architect of industrial policy, an arbiter of industrial problems and disputes and a regulator of industrial growth. Rather than managing the economy, it provides formal or informal "administrative guidance," backed up by strong statutory authority to intervene, coax or threaten. MITI is the most respected economic institution in Japan, enjoying the confidence of the business community in the soundness of its decisions. MITI also plays a leading role in agreements with Japanese industry to limit exports to various countries. The second most influential agency is JETRO (Japan External Trade Organization), founded in 1958.

A major Japanese contribution to international trade is the development of integrated general trading companies. First organized during the late 1800s, their role initially was to act as specialized wholesalers for Japanese manufacturers in domestic and foreign markets, often buying raw materials. Later they also served as financial intermediaries, engaging in direct investment. In addition, trading companies engage in trade among third countries, handling as many as 20,000 different products and as many suppliers. There are an estimated 6,000 trading companies in Japan, of which the top 10 have gross sales equal to 25% of Japan's GNP. The leading six firms are Mitsubishi, Mitsui, C. Itoh, Marubeni, Sumitomo and Nissho Iwai. Trading companies transact more than half the imports and exports. The Big Nine employ over 10,000 representatives abroad.

Export policy is based on the proposition "Export or perish" and was pursued for many years with single-minded tenacity. Japan's emergence as a major exporter after World War II was not easy. Foreign markets were both unfamiliar and hostile. Further, its exports started to receive most-favored-nation treatment from many GATT members (including the United Kingdom, France and Australia) only in the 1960s. Japan's strategy was twofold: first to develop world-class industries, and second to provide extensive export incentives.

Success in exports brought pressure on Japan to dismantle its carefully erected barriers against imports. The process of liberalization involved easing import quotas, reducing tariff rates, freeing transactions in foreign exchange and admitting foreign capital into the country. By 1964 Japan was able to achieve a level of liberalization required for full membership in GATT, IMF and OECD. However, not until December 1968 did it make the political decision truly to open its economy to international competition. Under the Kennedy Round of Multilateral Trade Negotiations completed in 1967, Japan reduced its tariff rates from 23.6% in 1968 to 11.2% in 1972 for consumer goods and from 15.2% to 9.3% over the same period for capital goods. Under the Tokyo Round of Multilateral Trade Negotiations concluded in 1979, Japan further reduced her tariff rates by 1987 on about 2,600 industrial products and about 200 agricultural and fishery products. In addition, it signed codes that called for the simplification of application procedures for import licenses, publication of standards for manufactured goods, setting of a customs valuation standard at sales price and government procurement based on nondiscrimination.

When the Tokyo Round tariff cuts are fully implemented, average tariff rates on industrial imports should decline to 2.5%, compared to 4.2% for the United States and 4.6% for the EEC. Tariffs are no longer serious bars to imports in Japan. In terms of import quotas, Japan still maintains quantitative restrictions on five manufactured goods and 22 agricultural products, down from 490 in 1962. However, the items under quota restrictions are the subject of considerable complaints from exporting countries. Japan is not the only country that imposes import quotas, but their stringency invites foreign criticism.

In contrast to the policy of eliminating gradually most import barriers in the industrial sector, protection remains strong in the agricultural sector. Agricultural import policy is determined mainly by the Ministry of Agriculture, Forestry and Fisheries, not by MITI. There is hardly any incentive to liberalize agricultural imports because Japan exports little; Japanese farmers are highly dependent on government price supports and have no hope of competing with foreign imports. As a result, Japanese food products are among the most expensive in the world.

Despite the opening up of the Japanese economy and a generally flexible trading policy, foreign firms are at a decided disadvantage in penetrating the domestic market. The invisible barriers include an unwieldy and intricate system of distribution that favors natives; complicated and time-consuming customs procedures; long time lags in regulatory approval; unexpected changes in standards; and the *zaibatsu* factor by which companies buy only from affiliated companies.

The growth of Japanese exports during the past 25 years has been phenomenal, rising from $4.1 billion in 1960 to $210.7 billion in 1986. In some years the export growth rate reached a high of 50%. The growth in exports was the result of both push and pull factors. The latter included the increasing demand for

Japanese products, their price-competitiveness and well-deserved reputation for quality and technical superiority, and the efficiency of Japanese overseas salesmen. The push factor came from the saturation of domestic markets, which made foreign markets the major outlets for an expanding industry. The Japanese also were skillful in shifting the composition of exports away from products subject to heavy competition toward products and goods in which it had technological dominance.

Imports have grown at a much slower pace, from $4.5 billion in 1960 to $127.5 billion in 1986. While exports grew by 6.4% from 1980 to 1986, imports grew by 3.5% during the same period. One factor in this growth has been the price of imports, which remained modest as a result of the appreciation of the yen. Another factor has been Japan's trade liberalization. The country imports a wide range of products, of which fuel, raw materials and food are the major items. Mineral fuels account for half of all imports, and food and raw materials for about 10% each. Categories of imports that declined as a percentage of imports over the 1960–80 period included soybean; wood; metal ores; chemicals; machinery; equipment; and textile materials including raw cotton and wool, the last of which declined from 17% to 1.7%. The predominance of imports of energy and raw materials implies that the process of import substitution has proceeded nearly as far as it can go. Generally, the products that Japan now imports have no domestic substitute. As raw materials and energy grow scarcer, Japan will be forced to conserve them and turn to higher-value-added exports.

Since 1963 Japan has not incurred a balance-of-trade deficit. However, Japanese balance-of-trade statistics overstate the value of imports and understate the value of exports since they are based on a customs clearance basis, not on a free-on-board basis, as in other countries. The customs value includes costs of shipping and insurance, which generally are included among imports and exports of services. Despite the appreciation of the yen, Japan had a positive balance of trade of $83.2 billion in 1986, compared with a deficit of $0.4 billion in 1960 and positive balances of $5.1 billion in 1972 and $18.2 billion in 1978. Although highly vulnerable to import price increases, Japan's strength lies in its ability to expand sales abroad correspondingly. This is partly attributable to the system of floating exchange rates, which automatically bring external accounts into balance.

On a broader balance on a current account basis, the Japanese performance is more mixed. Since 1961 the net service trade has been in deficit. Trade in services include transportation, insurance, travel expenditures and income from investments. The deficit also is influenced by the large outflow of funds from Japan for investment overseas, particularly in the United States.

In recent years capital flows have become important in terms of the balance of payments. Japan remained a net debtor nation until the mid-1960s. By 1967 total Japanese investments abroad began to exceed foreign investment in Japan, which changed it from a net debtor to a net creditor nation. Japan's major form or borrowing came in loans designed to assist domestic industrial development but gradually shifted more toward international sales of stocks. From 1945 to 1965 the government's investment policy was restrictive, and rigorous controls were placed on inflow and outflow of capital. In 1967 the government removed its restriction on international capital transactions. Until then, in principle, direct investment by foreign firms to establishing new businesses was forbidden, and the purchase of shares of existing businesses was restricted to 5% or less for one investor. In 1973 the law was amended to permit 100%-owned subsidiaries in all industries except for five. Seventeen additional industries were restricted to 50% foreign ownership. Limitations on the purchase of controlling shares of existing firms also were removed. In 1980 the new Foreign Exchange and Foreign Trade Control Law freed all external economic transactions except in rare instances of unusual instability in foreign exchange markets or abnormally large movements in funds.

Since 1964, when the balance of long-term capital flows turned negative, Japanese foreign investment has grown faster than foreign investment in Japan, reaching $400 billion in 1989. The bulk of foreign investment has gone into the United States. Throughout the 1980s this trend has been accelerating as a result of a number of factors, including the rising cost of land and labor in Japan, tightening pollution-control regulations, the desirability of reduced shipping costs for finished products as well as raw materials, circumvention of import quotas and tariff barriers, and availability of financial incentives from local governments in the form of reduced taxes or subsidies.

The Japanese bond markets also have been developing as sources of international financing. The first yen-denominated bond issue was floated by the Asian Development Bank in 1970, followed by similar issues by the World Bank and syndicates of Japanese banks. Japanese gold holdings were estimated in 1986 at 687 million g. (24.23 million oz.) and total reserves minus gold at 34.546 billion SDRs.

Japan trades with nearly every country in the world, but since the 1950s its export markets have been shifting from developing to developed countries. The United States is its largest trading partner, taking in 38% of its exports and supplying 17% of its imports. The United States is a major supplier of foodstuffs (including corn, wheat, fish, shellfish and meat), pulp, wood, chemicals, aircraft, office machinery, power-generating machinery, precision instruments, nonferrous metals, and toys and indoor games. In terms of exports, the United

States is Japan's largest customer of machinery and transportation equipment (28%), motor vehicles (44%), scientific and optical equipment, motorcycles, radio sets, television receivers, office machinery, metalworking machinery, recorders and watches. The balance of trade between the two countries runs heavily in favor of Japan. In 1987 Japan's exports to the United States were valued at $88.074 billion and imports at $28.249 billion. Such a lopsided trade and the consequent U.S. trade deficit ($59.825 billion) is a major point of friction between the two countries. It comprises a large portion of the overall U.S. trade deficit and has led to the erosion of U.S. free trade policies in the 1980s. Even more significantly, rapid incursions into U.S. markets by specific Japanese industries have caused political tensions. These have involved steel, television receivers, automobiles and computers. The United States has retaliated by placing numerous restrictions on further growth of the Japanese market shares, such as orderly marketing agreements, trigger price mechanisms and higher tariffs. Japan also has been persuaded to set voluntary restraints on exports of certain items such as automobiles and to increase its imports from the United States by liberalizing its trading sector and reducing many nontariff barriers to

FOREIGN TRADE INDICATORS 1986

Exports: $210.8 billion
Imports: $127.5 billion
Balance of trade: $83 billion
Annual growth rate, 1980–86 exports: 6.4%
Annual growth rate, 1980–86 imports: 3.5%
Ratio of international reserves to imports (in months): 3.6
Value of manufactured exports: $203.896 billion
Terms of trade (1980=100): 156 (1986)
Import Price Index (1980=100): 67.5 (1986)
Export Price Index (1980=100): 112.7 (1986)
Import of goods as % of GDP: 6.5
Export of goods as % of GDP: 10.7

Direction of trade (%)

	Imports	Exports
EEC	11.1	14.8
U.S.A.	23.1	38.8
East European economies	1.8	1.8

Composition of trade (%)

	Imports	Exports
Food / Agricultural raw materials	24.1	1.3
Fuels	6.4	0.3
Ores & minerals	29.4	0.2
Manufactured goods	40.1	98.2
of which chemicals	7.4	4.5
of which machinery	10.0	70.0

trade. Japan also has hurt U.S. sales in third-country markets and in developing countries, where the U.S. market share has shrunk from 36% to 22% and the Japanese share has grown from 11% to 25%.

Similar problems exist with Western Europe, where both the EEC and the EFTA record heavy annual balance-of-trade deficits. Exports have not only grown rapidly but also are concentrated in sensitive sectors. Japan's swift penetration of European markets for motor vehicles, television sets, integrated circuits and machine tools has caused considerable consternation among European manufacturers because Europeans have had a traditional dominance in these products.

In general, Japan has a trade surplus with every country in the world except oil exporters. Among the Communist countries, Japan's largest trading partners are China and the Soviet Union. Although Latin America accounts for only a small share of trade, it is an important region in Japan's strategy to diversify sources of energy and raw materials.

TRANSPORTATION & COMMUNICATIONS

Unlike transportation in other developed countries, Japan's transportation is characterized by the continuing importance of railways in passenger traffic. With 21,387 km. (13,292 mi.) of track—down from 27,880 km. (17,328 mi.) in 1965—Japan has the same density of rail network as France and Italy. Except on the Tokaido line, tracks throughout are narrow-gauge. Over 1,046 km. (650 mi.) are tunnels, and almost as many miles are spanned by bridges and viaducts. Following the elongated shape of the country, railways follow both coastlines, beginning at Aomori in northern Honshu as far as Lake Biwa, where the two lines meet. They continue side by side as far as Osaka, where they separate once again, one branch keeping to the shores of the Inland Sea. At Shimonoseki they join once more and cross over to Kyushu. The two trunk lines on Honshu are connected by a number of transverse lines that serve the interior. Honshu is connected with the island of Hokkaido by the Sei-Kan Tunnel, the longest in the world, and Honshu is connected with Shikoku by the Hon-Shi Bridge.

The flagships of the Japanese railway system are the four Shinkansen ("bullet train") lines—the Tokaido, the Sanyo, the Tohoku and the Joetsu. The Tokaido-Sanyo Shinkansen line was inaugurated in 1964, with an initial service connecting Tokyo and Shin-Osaka. The line was extended by stages. In 1972 the stretch of track connecting Shin-Osaka and Okayama was inaugurated, and in 1975 the remaining Okayama to Hakata portion, including a tunnel across Shimonoseki Strait, which separates Honshu and Kyushu. The 1,069-km.

(664-mi.) stretch from Tokyo to Hakata connects all major cities on the Pacific coast and is covered in less than six hours. The Shinkansen carries 10 million passengers a year and since 1964 has never suffered a major accident. The Tohoku and Joetsu lines were completed in 1982 and extend to Ueno. Most of the track is elevated, with banks in mountainous areas and viaducts in urban areas. In the case of the Sanyo Shinkansen, about half of the line runs through tunnels.

About 21% of the rail lines are run by private enterprises, mostly in the metropolitan areas around Tokyo, Osaka and Nagoya. The rest are operated by Japanese National Railways (JNR), which was split up in 1987 into six passenger railway companies, one national freight company and the Shinkansen Unit Holding Company. Management of the railways was transferred at the same time to a private body known as Japan Railway Group (JR). The most important consequence of the privatization was a reduction of the labor force in JR from 227,020 to 200,650.

Despite the efficiency of the rail system in metropolitan areas, with trains running every two minutes, the trains generally are overcrowded by as much as 250%. People are employed to push people into the compartments so that doors can close.

Subway services are operated by the Teito Rapid Transit Authority and the eight major municipalities of Tokyo, Sapporo, Yokohama, Nagoya, Kyoto, Osaka, Kobe and Fukuoka. The total length of the system in 1987 was 444.4 km. (276.2 mi.).

Road construction was not a priority with the government until the 1980s, and roads were neglected in favor of industry. The resulting traffic congestion is reflected in the fact that Japan had until the 1970s the highest accident rate per motor vehicle in the world. Only one-quarter of the roads were wide enough for two-lane traffic, and barely two-fifths had an asphalt or a cement surface. Of the prefectural roads, only 12% were paved. In the 1970s the first national highway system began to take shape, beginning with the 523-km. (325-mi.) expressway between Tokyo and Osaka. In 1987 there were 3,721 km. (2,313 mi.) of expressways, mostly running north to south.

The number of deaths and injuries from road traffic accidents has been increasing every year since 1980. In 1986 there were 579,190 road accidents involving automobiles in which 9,317 persons were killed and 712,330 injured. On the other hand, rail, maritime and aviation accidents have decreased since 1980.

Road haulage remains extensively regulated under a 1951 law that determines entry, exit, fares and activities. Licensees are divided into two categories: those operating on fixed routes and those operating in designated areas. Competing with these regulated haulers are a new breed of overnight package delivery services, parcel delivery services and couriers. Demand for these services has grown sixfold since 1981.

Japan has the third largest merchant fleet in the world. Even before the rise of other forms of transportation, coastal shipping was important as one of the main channels of domestic commerce. Roughly 51% of all merchandise shipped from one part of the archipelago to the other goes by sea, particularly bulk goods such as lumber and coal. Over 383 ferry services link isolated islands with the main ones. Japan has 1,100 ports, of which the 11 major ones handle 95% of international shipping.

TRANSPORTATION INDICATORS 1986

Roads
  Length, km. (mi.): 1,127,500 (700,600)
  Paved (%): 58

Motor vehicles
  Automobiles: 27,844,580
  Trucks: 17,139,806
  Persons per vehicle: 2.7
  Road freight, ton-km. (ton-mi.): 200.813 billion (137.546 billion)

Railroads
  Track, km. (mi.): 21,387 (13,292)
  Passenger-km. (passenger-mi.): 330.097 billion (205.101 billion)
  Freight, ton-km. (ton-mi.): 22.134 billion (15.061 billion)

Merchant marine
  Vessels: 10,011
  Total dead weight tonnage: 59,979,000
  Oil tankers: 1,267 (13,837,500 GRT)

Ports
  18 major (members of Japanese Port Association)
    114 other major ports
    2,000 minor ports
  Cargo loaded: 93,816,000 tons
  Cargo unloaded: 603,276,000 tons

Air
  Km. (mi.) flown: 337.1 million (234.1 million mi.)
  Passengers: 50,453,000
  Passenger-km. (passenger-mi.): 66.588 billion (41.376 billion)
  Freight-km. (freight-mi.): 3.784 billion (2.592 billion)
  Mail-ton-km.: 147.8 million (91.7 million ton-mi.)
  Airports with scheduled flights: 65
  Civil aircraft: 341 major aircraft

TRANSPORTATION INDICATORS 1986 *(continued)*

Pipelines
  Refined: 322 km. (200 mi.)
  Natural gas: 1,800 km. (1117.8 mi.)
  Crude: 84 km. (52.1 mi.)

Inland waterways
  Length, km. (mi.): 1,770 (1,100)
  Cargo, ton-km. (ton-mi.): 210.107 billion
    (143.912 billion)

COMMUNICATION INDICATORS, 1986

Telephones
  Total: 66,636,000
  Person per receiver: 1.8
  Phone traffic
    Local:
    Long distance: } 42 billion
    International: 253 billion

Post office
  Number of post offices: 23,615
  Domestic mail:
  Foreign mail received: } 17.160 billion
  Foreign mail sent:

Telegraph
  Total traffic: 41,154,000
  National: 40,560,000
  International: 794,000

Telex
  Subscriber lines: 47,000
  Traffic (000 minutes): 172,631

Telecommunications
  2 satellite ground stations

TOURISM & TRAVEL INDICATORS, 1986

Total tourist receipts: $1.137 billion
Expenditures by nationals abroad: $4.814 billion
Number of hotel beds: 153,000
Average length of stay: 11 days
Tourist nights: N.A.
Number of tourists: 2,036,000
  of whom from:
  U.S.A.: 461,300
  U.K.: 174,600
  West Germany: 43,400
  France: 28,800

Japan has three large airlines: Japan Air Lines (JAL), which handles international flights and domestic trunk routes; All-Nippon Airways (ANA), which handles domestic flights and international charters; and Japan Air System (JAS, formerly Towa Domestic Airlines), which flies mainly local routes. Formerly air transportation was subject to extensive regulation—airlines required licenses, and fare changes were subject to prior approval by the authorities. Growth in domestic air travel has been modest, with an 11% increase between 1980 and 1985 compared to 24% in the same period in the United States. The limitation of airport facilities, the availability of high-speed trains, and high air fares have tended to keep down air travel.

In an effort to deregulate the airline industry, JAL was privatized in 1987 through the sale of shares owned by the government; competition in the domestic market was encouraged by allowing more than one carrier; and ANA and JAS were allowed to service some international routes. Japan has 15 major international airports, including Tokyo's Narita International Airport. To relieve congestion at Narita, three new airport projects are under way: Kansai International Airport, the new Tokyo International Airport and the Tokyo International Airport Offshore development.

Telecommunications is dominated by Nippon Telegraph and Telephone Corporation (NTT), which was privatized in 1985. Reform of the telecommunications industry has consisted of both privatization and efforts to stimulate competition. The corporate status of NTT was changed to joint stock ownership, under which two-thirds of the shares are owned by the public and one-third by the government. Its new corporate status gave NTT the freedom to diversify into related fields and to exploit its technical expertise by establishing new subsidiaries. The domestic market has been opened to new carriers, divided into Type I and Type II, depending on the range of services provided.

DEFENSE

Japan's Self-Defense Forces (SDF), as the armed services are called, are the smallest among all the major industrial powers. Since 1945 they have been limited in size, structure and mission by a number of constitutional and informal restrictions, the most prominent of which is Article 9 of the Constitution, which states: "The Japanese people forever renounce war as a soveregn right of the nation or the threat or use of force as a means of settling international disputes." The SDF cannot be deployed outside the nation and are prohibited from possessing nuclear weapons or any arms with offensive capability. Since the end of World War II they have never seen action in any operation other than disaster relief. Further, they are under complete civilian control under the office of the prime minister. There is no formal Department of Defense or Defense High

Command. Against the background of prewar militarism, the nation has made a U-turn in military policy and adopted wholeheartedly a form of military passivism, or even pacifism, that is without parallel in modern history.

National security policy is based on the 1960 Treaty of Mutual Cooperation and Security with the United States, which extends to Japan the U.S. nuclear umbrella if ever required. International developments since the 1960s have called into question the wisdom of such a policy. The increasing vulnerability of ocean shipping on which the nation's foreign trade depends, the buildup of Soviet naval forces in the Pacific, the détente between the superpowers and the U.S. debacle in Vietnam have exposed Japan's need to develop the size and capability of its armed forces to defend the national territory. However, both public opinion and policymakers have opposed any significant move in this direction. Reaction to the prewar militarism still is strong. Economic motives also are strong in working against an increased defense capability. A reallocation of budgetary priorities in favor of defense would seriously curtail the government's concentration of resources on industrial development. Consequently defense expenditures are held below 1% of the GNP, the lowest among all industrial democracies.

The trauma of defeat has had a more permanent and profound impact on national attitudes than was apparent to outside observers in the immediate postwar period. The military elite were effectively excluded from public life and shorn of all influence. Disarmament was accepted with alacrity and enforced rigorously. Armament factories were dismantled, military schools were closed down and the General Staff was abolished. Even when in 1952, after the end of the Occupation, when the National Police Reserve was reconstituted as the National Safety Force under the National Safety Agency, Japan was careful to avoid the use of military terms to describe their organization and functions. Thus the army was called Ground Self-Defense Force (GSDF), the navy, the Maritime Self-Defense Force (MSDF) and their air force, the Air Self-Defense Force (ASDF).

Although the possession of nuclear weapons is not forbidden in the Constitution, Japan, as the only nation to suffer from atomic explosions in wartime, has consistently expressed its "nuclear allergy." The Basic Atomic Energy Law of 1956 limits research, development and utilization of atomic power to peaceful uses. The law's three "nonnuclear" principles prohibit the nation from possessing or manufacturing nuclear weapons or introducing them into the country. Even U.S. encouragement has not deflected the government from its resolve in this matter.

Although the SDF do not experience the same kind of hostility in the 1980s that they experienced in the 1950s and 1960s—when soldiers were turned away from public ceremonies and their children discriminated against in schools and on campuses—the SDF still are handicapped by the absence of a powerful military-industrial lobby. The ruling Liberal Democratic Party has adopted a policy of convenient ambivalence. While the SDF are viewed as a necessary evil, even the slightest evidence of their growth or concession to their interests evokes severe public reaction.

The statutory bases for the SDF are found in the Self-Defense Forces Law of 1954, the 1957 Basic Policy for National Defense and the 1976 National Defense Program Outline. The outline gave each force quotas of personnel and equipment for its tasks, and the specific elements of each force's mission were named. The tasks, however, are described with deliberate ambiguity and are not assigned any priorities. Essentially, the SDF are designed only to engage the attacker until the United States comes to Japan's aid. The policy illustrates Japan's extreme vulnerability in case of an actual invasion. Its small size, the geographical concentration of its industry and population, and the proximity of potentially hostile powers render the country virtually defenseless against a determined enemy or a nuclear strike. The terrain favors defenders against invaders, but protection of the long coastline would present unique problems.

Japan's defense establishment is unique in that it uses entirely nonmilitary nomenclature. The Defense Agency, as the supreme command is called, is under a director-general; he as well as his two principal assistants are civilians. The emperor has no connection with the SDF; he never reviews their units or visits their barracks. The ground, maritime and air forces are headed not by commanders but by staffs, the chiefs of which form the Joint Staff Council, the highest uniformed authority in the agency. The Diet intervenes in defense affairs through a defense committee and by debates on defense bills. Party lines on defense are clearly drawn, with only the Liberal Democratic Party clearly in favor of the status quo.

Two advisory bodies assist the prime minister in setting defense policies. The older is the National Defense Council, which meets rarely. The more effective one is the Ministerial Council on Overall Security Problems, which consists of the prime minister and a select group of ministers as well as the director-general of the defense agency. Basic policies and procedures are overseen by a number of internal bureaus, including the Defense Facilities Administration Agency. A number of auxiliary organs are attached to the Defense Agency, such as the National Defense College, the Defense Academy and the National Defense Medical College. The Technical Research and Development Institute is concerned with equipment and weapons. There are no military courts or military-justice codes. Military personnel, on or off duty, are subject to civil courts even when charged with offenses against national security. At every level, senior bureaucrats in the military establishment are drawn from the civilian sphere. Communication between commanders of each branch flows through civilian channels. Only in extreme emergencies are commanders permitted to act without direct authorization from the prime minister's office.

Demilitarization of national attitudes has been reinforced by educational programs emphasizing the subordination of the military to the civilian sector. Soldiers are required to keep a low profile, avoid sensitive political issues and eschew partisanship. Public school curricula do not extol the virtues of patriotism or of martial traditions. The Defense Agency also is constrained by poor logistics support and budgetary constraints. It did not have an independent communications system until 1983. Stockpiles of munitions are so low that they are expected to last for three to 10 days in an emergency.

The largest of the three forces is the GSDF, under the command of the chief of the ground staff. Although law permits a legal strength of 186,000, the force contains only 86% of that level, or approximately 160,000. It consists of one armored division, 12 infantry divisions, one artillery brigade, two antiaircraft artillery brigades, one airborne brigade, two composite brigades, one signal brigade, five engineer brigades, eight surface-to-air missile groups and one helicopter brigade. The GSDF is divided into five regional armies, each of which contains two to four divisions and an engineering brigade, antiaircraft artillery units and support units. The largest, the Northern Army, stationed in Hokkaido, has four divisions, including the only armored division; the Northeastern and Eastern armies, headquartered in Sendai and Ichikawa, respectively, each has two divisions; and the Central Army, headquartered in Itami, has three divisions in addition to a composite brigade. The Western Army, with two divisions, is headquartered at Kengun, with a composite brigade at Okinawa. The units are small; divisions are effectively of battalion strength and divisions of brigade strength. The ratio of officers to enlisted men is high—one to six—requiring the fleshing out of the units with volunteers in times of crisis. However, GSDF reserves receive little professional training.

Basic training lasts from 20 to 24 weeks; the second lieutenant candidate program for eight to 12 weeks. Advanced technical, flight, medical and command staff officer courses also are run by the GSDF.

The MSDF, with an authorized strength of 44,558, is commanded by a chief of the maritime staff, the only full admiral in the force. The force includes the self-defense fleet, five regional district commands, an air training squadron and various support units. The self-defense fleet, headquartered in Yokosuka, contains the fleet escort force; the fleet air force, with headquarters at Atsugi; two submarine flotillas; two mine-sweeping flotillas; and the fleet training commands. The five regional districts are at Ominato, Maizuru, Yokosuka, Kure and Sasebo. Training consists of three months' basic training for all recruits; two-year courses for flight students; six-month courses for officer candidates; and a one-year course for superior officers at Eta Jima, the site of the former Imperial Naval Academy. Like the GSDF, the MSDF suffers from weaknesses in critical areas, particularly logistics support and ship-based antiaircraft protection.

The ASDF, with an authorized strength 46,523, comprises the Air Defense Command; the Flying Training Wing; the Tactical Air Lift Wing; the Technical Training Command; and three independent wings for rescue, aircraft testing and air traffic control and weather operations. The Air Defense Command is divided into three regional air commands—Northern, Central and Western—in addition to the Southwestern Composite Air Wing, based at Naha in Okinawa. All regional headquarters control surface-to-air missile units of both the ADF and the GSDF in their respective areas. The ASDF maintains an integrated network of 28 radar installations and air defense direction centers known as the Basic Air Defense Ground Environment (BADGE). The ASDF has only limited capability to intercept enemy aircraft.

Recruitment to all three services is by voluntary enlistment. Although conscription is not banned, military service is abhorred by the younger generation, and recruiters are banned from university and college campuses. Predominantly rural prefectures supply most of the recruits, while urban areas, suffering labor shortages even in the civilian sector, supply few. Recruits may resign at any time, making retention a problem. Many are lured away by high-paying civilan jobs. Public-relations recruitment campaigns do not stress patriotism or national duty but rather benefits of learning a skill or keeping physically fit. The result is that Japan has one of the lowest civilian-to-soldier ratios among advanced countries. The defense budget, similarly, is the lowest among advanced countries both in terms of the GNP (below 1%) and the national budget (between 5% and 6%). But in view of Japan's large and growing GNP, it is difficult to use it as a yardstick; even below a minuscule 1% Japan has the world's eighth-largest military budget.

The Japanese defense forces are equipped almost entirely by domestic manufacturers. The only categories not domestically produced are artillery and high-performance strike aircraft. Japan is one of only eight countries to design, develop and produce its own tanks. The government budgets for defense procurement over a five-year period in what are known as the defense plans. The most important defense contractors are Mitsubishi, Kawasaki, Fuji, Ishikawajima-Harima and Nissan.

DEFENSE PERSONNEL, EQUIPMENT & BUDGET, 1987

Defense budget: $23.9 billion
% of national budget: 5
% of GNP: 1
per capita: $103.00
per soldier: $50,465
per sq km of national territory: $33,237
Total military manpower: 243,000
Reserves: Army: 43,000 Navy: 600
Armed forces per 1,000: 2

ARMY: 155,000 5 army headquarters (regional commands); 1 armored division, 12 infantry divisions; 2 composite brigades; 1 airborne brigade; 1 artillery brigade; 1 signals brigade; 5 engineer brigades
NAVY: 44,000 (including Naval Air)
Bases: Yokosuka, Kure, Sasebo, Maizuru, Ominato
AIR FORCE: 44,000 270 combat aircraft; 3 fighter squadrons; 10 interceptor squadrons; 1 reconnaissance squadron; 6 combat air wings, 1 combat air group.
Arms Imports: $702 million
Arms Exports: $84 million

Both the services and the combat dress are American in style. The U.S. helmet is worn. Arms of service wear distinctive colors as piping, while the cap badge insignia displays the dove of peace.

EDUCATION

The Japanese are the most literate people in Asia, with virtually 100% literacy. Even as far back as the Tokugawa period, Japan had a literacy rate of 40% to 50% for males and 15% for females. Although formal schools did not exist then, there were centers of Buddhist and Confucian learning, catering mainly to the upper classes. But the modern system of education began to take shape only since 1872, when under the Meiji Restoration's reformist influence the Fundamental Code of Education (Gakusei) was adopted. Under the code, education became universal and compulsory, organized in progressive steps from elementary school to university. Modeled after that of France, the system was placed under the strong central control of the Ministry of Education. The entire country was divided into eight educational districts, with a university in each district. With the aid of an American adviser, David Murray, normal schools were established for training teachers. Tokyo University , the first Western-style university, was established in 1877. The first school for handicapped children was founded in 1878. As a result of these efforts, nearly 90% of Japanese children received some form of education by the turn of the century.

Rising reaction against alien influences—American, French and Prussian—in the school system led to the issuance in 1890 of the *Imperial Rescript on Education*, which sought to restore the authenticity of traditional national values, including *shushin* (moral education) and *kokutai* (national polity). Combining Shinto emperor worship and Confucian values of loyalty, filial piety and obedience, the rescript served as the guiding rudder of the educational system until 1945: It performed a dual function of promoting modernization and maintaining social order and control. After 1930 the rescript was used as an instrument to check intellectual ferment and rouse nationalism. The system was strongly centralized and elitist, universal in its primary levels but highly selective in its secondary and higher stages. From the 1930s secondary schools were geared more closely to the needs of expansionist policies. Compulsory military training was introduced, and authoritarian control over education was strengthened by the establishment of the Bureau of Thought Control in the Ministry of Education.

This period of educational history came to an end with Japan's defeat in 1945. Under the Allied Occupation, an effort was made to democratize Japanese education by removing militaristic and ultranationalistic educators from the system. A series of educational reforms followed based on the recommendations of the U.S. Educational Mission led by George D. Stoddard. The *Imperial Rescript on Education* was rescinded. American-style social studies, with emphasis on democratic citizenship, replaced *shushin*. Central control was diluted by creating local and prefectural boards of education. The Imperial University and its elite feeder higher schools were abolished. Compulsory education was extended from six to nine years and an American-style 6-3-3-4 school ladder was established. Although many of these reforms were modified in the years following the end of the Occupation, their core features have survived to this day.

Unlike the U.S. Constitution, the Japanese Constitution makes specific reference to education, in Article 26, which makes education a right of the people. Another legacy of the Occupation period is the Fundamental Law of Education, passed by the Diet in 1947. It affirms the guiding principles that characterize Japanese education, with academic freedom, equal opportunity and religious neutrality among them. Other Occupation laws dealing with education included the School Education Law of 1947, the Board of Education Law of 1948 and the Ministry of Education Establishment Law and the Private School Law of 1949. Some of these laws have been replaced or revised. In 1956 the Law Concerning the Organization and Functions of Local Educational Administration began a recentralization trend by having school board members appointed rather than popularly elected. There also was a swing back from comprehensive

schools to specialized secondary schools and a reintroduction of moral education, now called *dotoku kyoiku.*

The academic year begins in April and ends in March. In both elementary
and lower secondary schools the school year is divided into three terms: April
to July, September to December and January to March. Upper secondary
schools have either a two- or a three-term school year, while universities follow
a two-semester system. On average, a student spends 225 days in school every
year. The school-week is five and a half days long, including Saturday.

Japanese education is examination-oriented, and entrance examinations govern the educational cycle. Standardized tests have been in use since 1948 in
schools and since 1979 in colleges and universities. Achievement tests are administered by the prefectures. In noting pupils' performance, school records in-
dicate not only their relative position in class but also the extent of their attain-
ment of a set target in each subject. Tutoring schools specializing in training
pupils to pass examinations are very popular.

The role of private and religious schools varies with the level of education. At
the compulsory level it is very slight, accounting for less than 1% of the enrollment. It is highest at the kindergarten level, where the percentage of enrollment
is over 73%, and at the university level, where it is 76%. In the noncompulsory
upper secondary schools the percentage is 28%, but in technical colleges it is
less than 1%. Private schools are run primarily by religious institutions but also
include ethnic schools and schools for foreign communities. Private schools
charge tuition, just as public secondary schools do, but receive government subsidies covering part of their expenditures. A large majority of the lower secondary schools provide free lunches.

The first *yochien* (kindergarten) was founded in Japan in 1876 and attached
to the Tokyo Women's Normal School (now Ochanomizu University). Since
that time, kindergartens have flourished, accepting children aged tree, four and
five. Kindergartens are regulated by education authorities; day care centers, by
public welfare authorities. Admission to the more prestigious kindergartens is
so competitive that there are schools that prepare the toddlers for the entrance
tests!

Primary schooling *(shoogakko)* lasts for six years, from age six. Primary
schools throughout the country are fairly uniform in standards and practices,
except in isolated mountainous areas. The most striking trend is the increasing
use of *juku* (supplementary nonformal tutorial schools). Nine subjects are offered at the primary level, including Japanese, social studies, arithmetic,
science, music, arts, crafts, physical education and homemaking.

Secondary schooling is divided into a compulsory three-year segment known
as lower secondary school *(chugakko)*, and a three-year, noncompulsory seg-

ment known as upper secondary school *(kotogakko)*, or grades seven through nine and ten through twelve, respectively. There are no leaving examinations at the end of the lower secondary level, and generally all children advance to the next level. More differentiated than primary school or lower secondary school, upper secondary school offers students the opportunity to branch out in different directions. In lower secondary school, 1,500 class hours are designated each year, divided into the same nine subjects as in primary school. Foreign language is an elective, but almost all students study English. Thirty-five class hours are devoted each year to moral education. Students are expected to have learned the 1,945 standard Chinese characters *(kanji)* at the completion of grade nine. More than one-third of the upper secondary schools offer only general courses, another one-third are comprehensive schools offering general and specialized courses, and another one-third offer only vocational and specialized programs. Curricular standards are based on the number of credits, a credit being equivalent to 35 50-minute segments. English is offered as a second language.

Vocational education is offered at five-year technical colleges (which admit graduates of lower secondary schools), government-sponsored vocational training centers and "miscellaneous schools' outside the regular school system.

The upper secondary equivalent of the *juku* is the *yobiko*, privately run preparatory schools that help students pass the university entrance examinations. There are close to 300 *yobiko* in the country, with tuition charges in many cases exceeding those of the colleges. The *yobiko* administer mock university entrance examinations based on previous examinations. Professors at leading universities are employed by these institutions at competitive salaries. The top one, such as Yoyogi Seminar and Surugudai, have facilities comparable to those of the great universities.

Tokyo University, founded in 1877, is Japan's oldest university and was the harbinger of higher education. In 1886 it was named an imperial university, thus placing it as the capstone of the educational system. Six more imperial universities were established during the period up to the start of World War II: Kyoto (1897), Tohoku (1907), Kyushu (1910), Hokkaido (1918), Osaka (1931) and Nagoya (1939). The University Code of 1918 recognized private, municipal and prefectural universities in addition to the imperial ones. The imperial universities did not admit women as students, and they were therefore forced to enroll at private universities. Prestigious private universities include Waseda and Keio, both in Tokyo. The two major Christian universities are Doshisha in Kyoto and International Christian University in Tokyo. The best-known Buddhist university is Ryukoku in Kyoto.

Not only has Japan a large proportion of its students in higher education, but also university graduation has a mystique that is rarely found elsewhere to the same degree. Japanese society has been described as a *gakureki shakai* (education record) society and the Japanese ruling class as a degreeocracy. Even more important than the degrees themselves is the prestige of the granting institution. Having an extremely hierarchical society, the Japanese have ranked their educational institutions in an elaborate pecking order. Students and their parents expend superhuman efforts to get into the top universities in the same way that a samurai sought a master. Thus the term *ronin* (masterless samurai) is applied to these students.

Under the law, universities have considerable autonomy in the general management of their affairs. Universities are made up of one or more faculties (sometimes called colleges or schools), each of which, in turn, is made up of departments. Departments are organized either by the "chair" system (where research is emphasized) or the "subject" system (where teaching is emphasized). Each chair, usually made up of a professor, an assistant professor and an assistant, has its own budget. Most private universities are organized according to the subject system. The faculty council elects the president and the deans in the national universities and in many private universities. Faculty and staff in public universities are civil servants. Tuition at public universities is generally lower than that at private ones. National universities are almost wholly funded by the government, while private universities receive about a quarter of their revenues from public subsidies.

Junior colleges were established in 1948 to give introductory training in liberal arts and were called short-course universities. They tend to specialize in home economics, teacher training and the humanities. Most offer two-year courses, and their credits are transferable toward a bachelor or arts degree.

Once admitted, the students find progress smooth. Approximately three-quarters of the students complete their studies in four years. Most of the classes are lectures, and seniors need not attend any classes except the final examination. A graduation thesis is in many cases the only other requirement. Because there is little competition, most institutions do not offer special awards for scholarship. Universities are diploma factories, providing the desired degree with minimal effort and entrée into the job market. Students generally stay with the department or faculty in which they are enrolled, and transfers are infrequent. The first two years are spent in general courses, followed by specialized courses in the last two. The credit system is used, with one credit equivalent to a lecture class of one hour per week (or two hours for a seminar and three hours for laboratory work) for a 15-week semester. A four-year university program calls for 124 credits. Professional courses require five to six years of study. The only official graduate degrees are master's and the doctorate. More than

155 universities offer doctoral-level programs. There has been a rise in the number of specialized universities and institutions for advanced research.

A new breed of university teachers, described as *sararimen*, work only from nine to five and remain aloof from the students. This contrasts with the traditional Japanese professor, who devotes all his time and energies to the students and university work. One fundamental aspect of the university system is the veneration in which the professor is held by his students, and his paternalistic attitude toward them. The relationship is so close that it continues after the student has left academe. Students continue to visit and seek advice from their former professor and even publish memorial volumes in his honor after his death. Professors enjoy considerable academic freedom and are free to form unions and become active politically.

Student activism has been a well-established tradition in Japanese universities since Meiji times, when the great imperial universities were centers of resistance to official ideology. Marxism took strong roots there in the immediate postwar period, turning them into strongholds of iconoclasm. Marxism remains strong, especially among the faculty, but its influence is waning. Despite revolutionary rhetoric, modern student activism is not necessarily motivated by ideology. The public and the press have customarily regarded student strikes and demonstrations as predictable student behavior compounded more of romantic exuberance and opposition to authority than as an expression of political commitment. Under university regulations, striking students could be expelled, placed on probation or admonished, but these measures have seldom been employed, except against leaders in flagrant cases. The tolerance of the school authorities is typically matched by the indifference of the public to periodic student uproars. Often the student radicals turn into conservative employees and pillars of the establishment upon emergence from the campus chrysalis.

Student activism reached its peak in the late 1960s under the leadership of the All-Japan Federation of Student Self-Government Associations (Zengakuren), formed in 1948 on the initiative of the Japanese Communist Party. Together with another nonsectarian group called Joint Struggle Committee (Zenkyoto), it waged an all-out struggle in campus and street battles from 1968 to 1969. The movement finally collapsed in 1971. The hard-core radicals reappeared in such groups as the Red Army Faction, while other radicals turned to the Green Movement. The movement never recovered its strength, partly because of factional struggles; partly because the reforms demanded by the activists had been gradually implemented; and partly because of the growing affluence of the society, which inhibited dissidence. Some students have turned instead to religious activism, with the student arm of the Soka Gokkai steadily gaining in strength since the 1970s.

The Ministry of Education, Science and Culture (Mombusho), commonly known as the Ministry of Education, is the central government agency in charge of education. Since the 1950s the ministry has reversed the decentralization of educational administration initiated under the Occupation and amassed more powers over educational institutions. The ministry also has jurisdiction over "social education," including such facilities as libraries, museums and audiovisual centers. The ministry's work is supported by a number of advisory councils, of which the most prominent is the Central Council of Education, formed in 1952 by the reorganization of the former Education Reform Council.

Boards of education operate at the prefectural and municipal levels. The prefectural governor appoints members of the prefectural board with the approval of the prefectural legislature, and mayors appoint municipal boards with the consent of the respective councils. Municipal and prefectural superintendents of schools are appointed by the respective boards. Public elementary and lower secondary schools are operated by the municipal boards of education, while public special schools and upper secondary schools are run by the prefectural boards.

The major source of educational funds is the central government, which underwrites two-thirds of all school expenditures. National schools and universities are directly financed by the Ministry of Education. Local school finances are shared by the Ministry of Education and the Ministry of Home Affairs on the one hand and prefectures and municipalities on the other. The national government pays half the salaries of teachers in public schools, and the prefectures pay the other half.

What is ordinarily known as adult education is known in Japan by the more general term "social education," encompassing education outside the formal system for both adults and children. It is under the jurisdiction of the Ministry of Education, which directly operates facilities as citizens' public halls, providing lectures and exhibitions. Continuing education for adults returning to school for further studies is not well developed. Most adult students enroll in night courses. Upper secondary school diplomas can be earned by correspondence courses or by radio and television courses. Of special note is the NHK Gakuen, run by the Japan Broadcasting Corporation, the national public network. The national government-supported Broadcast College, patterned after the British Open University, was established in 1983.

Teaching is a respected profession in Japan, as is to be expected in a society with an abiding faith in education. Teachers in primary school and schools for handicapped children are trained in teachers' colleges, while secondary school teachers attend regular universities. Kindergarten teachers, who are mostly women, are trained in private junior colleges and in Ministry of Education institutes. By law, all teachers must have teaching certificates. First-class certificates require a bachelor's degree for teachers in kindergarten, primary and lower secondary school and a master's degree for teachers in upper secondary school. Second-class certificates require a junior college diploma, except for teachers in upper secondary school, for whom a bachelor's degree is required. Teachers are required to participate from time to time in in-service education programs. Teachers in schools affiliated with the national universities are appointed by the Ministry of Education; others, by prefectural or municipal boards of education. Teachers gain tenure after the first six months of teaching. Although salary scales vary with the prefecture, they are generally higher than for comparable civil servants.

Teaching is one of the most heavily unionized professions, with over 69% of the teachers belonging to unions. The largest is the Japan Teachers' Union (JTU or Nikkyoso), which claims 52% of the teachers and has a membership of over 500,000. Heavily radical and left-wing, it has two factions, one aligned with the Japan Socialist Party and the other with the Japanese Communist Party.

EDUCATION INDICATORS 1986

Literacy
  Total (%): 100
  Males (%): 100
  Females (%): 100

First level
  Schools: 24,933
  Students: 10,226,325
  Teachers: 448,978
  Student–teacher ratio: 22.8
  Net enrollment rate: 100
  Females (%): 49

Second level
  Schools: 16,738
  Students: 11,456,437
  Teachers: 566,976
  Student–teacher ratio: 20.2
  Net enrollment rate: 95
  Females (%): 49

Vocational
  Schools:
  Students: 1,381,000
  Teachers:
  Student–teacher ratio:

EDUCATION INDICATORS 1986 *(continued)*

Vocational enrollment rate:

Third level
  Institutions: 1,097
  Students: 2,597,073
  Teachers: 138,587
  Student–teacher ratio: 18.7
  Gross enrollment rate: 29.6
  Graduates per 100,000 ages 20–24: 2,006
  % of population over 25 with postsecondary
    education: 14.3
  Females (%): 34

Foreign study
  Foreign students in national universities: 10,697
  Students abroad: 14,297
    of whom in
      U.S.A.: 11,248
      France:
      West Germany: 1,128
      U.K.: 322

Public expenditures
  Total: Yen 15.050 trillion (1982)
  % of GNP: 5.7
  % of national budget: 19.1
  % current:

Graduates 1983

Total: 576,487
Education: 66,985
Humanities & religion: 94,922
Fine & applied arts: 19,814

Law: N.A.
Social & behavioral sciences: 166,123
Commerce & business: N.A.

Mass communication: N.A.
Home economics: 55,715
Service trades: N.A.

Natural sciences: 10,958
Mathematics & computer science: 3,580
Medicine: 29,091

Engineering: 94,967
Architecture: N.A.
Industrial programs: N.A.

Transportation & communications: 617
Agriculture, forestry, fisheries: 16,138
Other: 17,577

LEGAL SYSTEM

Article 76 to the Constitution assigns the "whole judicial power" to the Supreme Court and various inferior courts. This means that no executive organ partakes of this power. The Supreme Court alone determines the procedures, practices and administration of all courts. The inferior courts prescribed in the Constitution are the eight high courts and 49 district courts, with 235 branches and 570 summary courts. There also are 49 family courts with 235 branches.

The chief judge of the Supreme Court is designated by the cabinet and appointed by the emperor. Imperial appointment endows the chief judge with a prestige comparable to that of the prime minister. The 14 other judges are appointed by the cabinet subject to popular review at the first House of Representatives election after the appointment and every 10 years thereafter. If they disapprove, the judge is dismissed. Actually, no judge has ever been voted out of office. The Supreme Court renders its decisions either from a full bench or from petty benches of five justices each. Full benches are required for decisions on cases involving constitutionality, on cases without precedent, on cases in which the decision of the petty bench ended in a tie and on cases of special importance. The court includes 20 research clerks, themselves experienced judges.

The functions of the Supreme Court reflect the constitutional emphasis on the independence of the judiciary. It is the court of last resort for civil and criminal cases. It also is responsible for the administration of the entire court system, promulgating procedural rules, assigning judges to specific courts, appointing and removing court officials other than judges, preparing court budgets and making rules for public prosecutors. The Supreme Court also prepares the list from which the cabinet appoints judges. Article 81 of the Constitution gives the Supreme Court the power of judicial review; it can declare laws, official acts and administrative rules unconstitutional, although it rarely does so.

High courts function as courts of appeal in civil and criminal cases and also have original jurisdiction in election cases. These courts use a collegiate system of benches, consisting of from three to five judges. District courts have original jurisdiction in all civil and criminal cases except for petty offenses. They also hear appeals from summary courts. Most cases are heard by one judge, and complicated cases by three judges. On the lowest rung of the judicial ladder are the summary courts, which try minor civil and criminal cases by summary procedure and issue warrants for arrest, seizure and search. Family courts are on a level with district courts and have original jurisdiction in matters concerning inheritance, divorce and juvenile delinquency.

The criminal justice system is based on the Penal Code of 1860 (substantially revised in 1907) and the Code of Criminal Instruction of 1880, both based on French models. A legal revolution took place with the promulgation in 1949 of the new Code of Criminal Procedure, sponsored by the Occupation authorities. The code guarantees explicitly the fundamental rights of the citizen and favors the defendant over the accuser. More significantly, it abolished the feudal concept of the family as the basic social unit and established substantial equality of the sexes. Equally important were reforms in civil procedure whereby parties examine evidence in place of preliminary investigation by the court, and cross examination replaces examination solely by the judge. Nevertheless, Japanese courts have retained many traditional features. Thus the trial judge tends to play a more active role than does his counterpart in an American court. There are frequent and informal discussions between the judge and counsel. The present Constitution does not provide for a jury system.

Corresponding to each court at every level are public procurators, who represent the state in criminal cases. The procurators are civil servants under the control and supervision of the Ministry of Justice. Institutional safeguards check the procurator's discretionary powers of nonprosecution. Committees of laypersons are established in conjunction with branch courts to hold inquests on a procurator's decisions. They meet four times yearly and may issue orders for a case to be reinvestigated and prosecuted. Victims or interested parties also may appeal a decision not to prosecute.

The Criminal Code sets minimum and maximum sentences for offenders. Penalties range from fines and short-term incarceration to compulsory labor and the death penalty. Heavier penalties are meted out for recidivists and for offenses against parents. Capital punishment consists of death by hanging and may be imposed on those convicted of leading an insurrection, inducing or aiding foreign armed aggression, arson or homicide.

Western-style penology was adopted in Japan during the Meiji period. The Prison Law of 1908 provided the first attempt to codify rules and regulations regarding prison administration. It stipulated separate facilities to house those sentenced to confinement with labor, without labor and those detained for trial or for short sentences. The Juvenile Law of 1922 established administrative organs to deal with offenders under age 18 and officially recognized voluntary workers as a major element in the community-based treatment of juveniles. Parole and probations systems for adults were established after World War II.

The Correctional Bureau of the Ministry of Justice is responsible for the administration of the adult prison system, the juvenile correctional system and three women's guidance homes, while the ministry's Rehabilitation Bureau operates the probation and parole systems.

A relatively high proportion of the prison population are repeat offenders. The penal system is designed to resocialize, reform and rehabilitate offenders. Vocational and formal education are emphasized, as is instruction in social values. Most convicts are engaged in labor, for which a small stipend is paid or set aside for use on release. Prison privileges are based on good behavior. Noninstitutional sentences are used extensively to substitute for or to supplement prison terms. A large number of those given suspended sentences by judges are released to the supervision of volunteer officers under the guidance of professional probation officers.

LAW ENFORCEMENT

Japan's first civil police force was established in 1871 and was modeled along continental European lines. After the nation's defeat in 1945, the Occupation authorities introduced in 1947 a new Police Law, decentralizing the force by creating approximately 1,600 municipal forces alongside rural police under prefectural control. Civilian control was assured by placing the police under the jurisdiction of public safety commissions under the National Public Safety Commission in the office of the prime minister. The Home Ministry was abolished and the police were stripped of their responsibility for fire protection, public health and other administrative duties.

The decentralized system soon was found to be unwieldy, inefficient and expensive. Small municipalities could not support police departments, and local bosses and gangsters exerted undue influence on police activities. As a result, the law was amended in 1951 to allow smaller communities to merge with the National Rural Police, and most opted to do so. The law was again amended, in 1954, for a final restructuring under which local forces were consolidated by prefectures under the National Police Agency. The Public Safety Commission was retained. National standards were established regarding training, pay, uniforms, rank and promotion.

The National Police Agency is under the direct control of the National Public Safety Commission, which can appoint or dismiss senior police officers. The commission consists of a chairman who holds the rank of a minister of state, and five members appointed by the prime minister with the consent of the Diet. The National Police Agency, the supreme operational authority, is under the direction of a commissioner-general. The agency's central office includes a number of bureaus dealing with administration, criminal investigation, public safety, communications, traffic and security. The Security Bureau conducts research into equipment and tactics in suppressing riots. It also is responsible for surveillance of aliens and radical political groups.

The National Police Agency maintain 11 regional police bureaus, each responsible for an area consisting of several prefectures. Metropolitan Tokyo and Hokkaido are excluded from the jurisdiction of the regional bureaus and are run more autonomously than other local forces, the former because of its urban nature and the latter because of special geographical conditions. The National Police Agency also directly controls the Imperial Guard, the National Research Institute of Police Science and the National Police Academy.

Local police systems encompass 45 prefectural police forces in addition to the Tokyo Metropolitan Police and the Hokkaido Prefectural Police. They have limited initiative. Not only are the most important activities regulated by the National Police Agency, but it also pays for equipment, escort, natural disaster duties and antiriot operations. The strength and rank allocation of local personnel as well as the location of local police stations are established by National Police Agency statutes. The prefectures finance and control the policemen on the beat, criminal investigation, traffic control and other duties.

Prefectural public safety commissions supervise police agencies within their respective jurisdictions. These bodies, the eight larger ones consisting of five members and the others of three members each, are appointed by the prefectural governor with the consent of the assemblies. The Tokyo Metropolitan Police is the only force to be headed by a superintendent-general instead of a public safety commission. Each prefectural police force is divided into districts (and in larger jurisdictions, substations). Below them are police boxes, equal to U.S. precincts, which form the first line of police response to the public. Police boxes in urban areas are manned by several officers, who conduct foot patrols while on duty. In rural areas police boxes are manned by a single policeman, who lives with his family in adjacent quarters. Patrolmen in police boxes have intimate knowledge of their jurisdictions. In fact, most police boxes look like ordinary homes and cottages in rural areas and may be found in the most strange settings in urban areas: above bars, on traffic islands, beside underpasses or in the arcades of railway stations. Wherever they are found, they have a red-light globe hanging over their front door. Because of the congestion of Japanese streets, only a minority of patrolmen work in cars.

While on patrol the demeanor of the Japanese policeman is self-effacing, low-key and unauthoritarian. He does not swagger or posture and often is as inconspicuous as a mailman. In conformity with social mores, he avoids eye contact with people unless specifically obligated to do so. In stature the Japanese policeman is among the smallest among advanced countries: The required minimum height is only 1.6 m. (5 ft., 3 in.) and the weight 54 kg. (119 lb.). But the absence of imposing physical bulk is more than made up by skills in hand-to-hand combat. Their martial arts techniques often are more effective than handguns. Because restraint and reserve are highly valued traits in Japanese society, the policeman who forbears use of physical violence or force is highly admired.

Police work is almost entirely a male profession in Japan. Women have been recruited only since 1946, and they are employed only in the largest 17 prefectures at more lowly jobs, such as counselling juveniles and looking for shoplifters and pickpockets. Some prefectures have female traffic personnel who are not sworn officers.

One of the primary police tasks is to conduct a twice-yearly house-to-house residential survey of homes and business in the area, recording all vital information on cards that are then stored and filed in the police box. Participation in the survey is voluntary, but most citizens cooperate except for leftists.

Police discipline is extremely high, and instances of misbehavior or brutality are rare. Many reasons have been cited for the high standards of personal conduct among policeman. In addition to institutional mechanisms such as the Human Rights Bureau and the civilian board of review in public safety commissions, there is a powerful and pervasive Confucian ethic of social propriety that sustains responsible police behavior. Police work is not only less demanding but also less dangerous. Firearms play a negligible part in crime; less than 16 handguns are involved per 100,000 offenses. Policemen do not have to fear sharpshooters or fiery ambushes. On an average less than five officers are killed annually in the line of duty and hardly ever by firearms.

Japanese policemen are one of the hardest-working groups of a hardworking people. The hours of police work are irregular as well as long. Most patrolmen are on duty for 56 hours a week in the so-called three-shift system in which they work one day from 9:00 A.M. to 5:30 P.M. and the next day from 8:30 A.M. to the following morning at 10:00 A.M. Policeman are given 20 days of vacation each year, but few take them. During working hours policemen display a great deal of punctilio. They rarely take off their hats in public or inside the boxes and invariably put on white gloves while on duty. Their uniform is extremely formal, except in summer. It consists of a four-button double-breasted coat worn over a white shirt and tie. In winter the coat and trousers are black; in spring and autumn, steel blue. A Sam Browne belt is worn over the jacket. In summer they shed their coat and tie and wear an open-necked steel-blue shirt with matching trousers. The police cap is peaked in front, with a short black visor. On the front above the visor is the gold emblem of the police, a five-pointed star enclosed by pine branches. Rank insignia are worn on coat lapels or breast pockets. Patrolmen generally wear ankle-length boots. There are neither identifying numbers nor name tags. Every policeman carries with him standardized equipment: a 38-caliber revolver in a holster attached to the right shoulder by a lanyard; handcuffs in a rear left belt pouch; a nightstick with a leather thong down the left leg; a small radio receiver in the breast pocket; and in a trouser pocket a light 4.6-m. (15-ft.) rope used for the ancient rope-tying art of *hojo*.

Within their security divisions, each prefectural police and the Tokyo Metropolitan Police maintain a branch manned with special riot units who are used in crowd control during violent public demonstrations or festivals. In handling the former, riot units are employed en masse, military-style. They line streets, standing shoulder to shoulder, three or four deep. Operations are carried out by units of nine- to 11-man squads, 27-1 to 33-man platoons and 80- to 100-man companies. Front ranks are trained to open to allow passage of special squads to rescue captured police or to engage in tear gas assaults. The riot police are committed to using disciplined, nonlethal force and carry no firearms. They show great poise under stress and listen to taunting crowds for hours without losing their temper. The riot police have special dress and equipment: body armor, including a corselet hung from the waist, aluminum down the backbone, shoulder pads, armored gauntlets, helmets with faceplates and padded skirts down the back to protect the neck; and 1.2-m. (4-ft.) shields. Riot police live in virtually self-sufficient compounds. Training is constant, with military-style mock battles. However, duty as a riot policeman is not popular, since it entails constant training and much boredom between irregularly spaced assignments.

In addition to the regular police, there are numerous other police agencies handling specialized police functions. These include the Maritime Safety Agency of the Ministry of Transportation; the railway police; immigration agents; postal inspectors; revenue inspectors of the Ministry of Finance; and police units in charge of forest preservation, narcotics control, fishery inspection and mine safety.

There are 11 ranks in the police force. In descending order they are: commissioner-general, superintendent-general, superintendent supervisor, chief superintendent, senior superintendent, superintendent, police inspector, assistant police inspector, police sergeant, senior policeman and policeman. Senior officers over the rank of chief superintendent are given the same salary and allowances as regular public service personnel, while officers below that rank are covered by a compensation system based on seniority, education and rank. Opportunities for career advancement are greater in Japan than in the United States. Almost one-third of policemen hold a rank higher than that of patrolman. There also is constant circulation of staff to prevent units from becoming ingrown.

Entry into the police force is made at two levels: patrolman and assistant inspector. The first is conducted separately by each prefecture and the second on a national basis by the National Police Agency. Police work tends to attract the more conservative youth. Although the Constitution prohibits job discrimination on the basis of political beliefs or affiliations, the police reject applicants with antisocial (i.e., left-wing) tendencies.

Metropolitan or prefectural police schools conduct education and training for newly recruited officers, while regional police schools conduct education for officers who are to be promoted to the rank of police sergeant or assistant police inspector. The National Police Academy trains newly appointed police inspectors. The Higher Training Institute for Investigative Leaders is a special institute for investigation officers in command positions.

Crimes are divided into six main categories: felonies, violent offenses, larceny, intellectual offenses, moral offenses and miscellaneous offenses. Felonies, the most serious, comprise murder, robbery, rape and arson; violent offenses include unlawful assembly and possessing dangerous weapons, simple and aggravated assault, extortion and intimidation; larceny comprises burglary, vehicle theft and shoplifting; intellectual crimes include fraud, embezzlement, counterfeiting, forgery, bribery, and breach of trust; moral offenses comprise gambling and pornography; and miscellaneous offenses include obstruction of official duties, unauthorized entry, death or injury caused by negligence, possession of stolen property and destruction of property. Special laws define miscellaneous offenses, such as prostitution; illegal possession of swords or firearms; customs violations; and possession of various controlled substances, such as marijuana. Of the annual crime total, 5% are felonies, 86% larcenies and 9% the remainder. This rate represents the lowest rate of criminal activity among advanced countries. In fact, violent crime is only a fraction of what it is in Europe and the United States. Tokyo has the well-deserved reputation of being the safest of all the world's major metropolitan areas.

Western observers analyzing Japan's low crime rate have identified a number of contributory factors, of which the most powerful is a sense of shame or losing face from not conforming to expectations of conduct and discharging social rights and obligations toward the group to which one belongs. Others are just as important. Japan is essentially a homogeneous society that places a premium on unemotional behavior in public, restraint in conduct and poise under stress. The economy is prosperous, and there are no great pockets of dire poverty. There is a strict and effective weapons control law regulating possession and sale of handguns, rifles and other firearms. Almost all crimes committed with firearms are carried out by members of criminal gangs. What astonishes many criminologists is the fact that despite rapid urbanization and modernization, the crime rates have tended to go down and not up, as in other countries experiencing similar demographic trends.

Nevertheless, Japan is not entirely free of criminal problems in specific areas. The most severe law enforcement problems involve narcotics abuse, white-collar crime, juvenile delinquency and organized crime. All these conditions are characteristic of postindustrial societies and Japan is no nearer a solution to these problems than the United States is. Organized crime particularly has assumed massive proportions, keeping pace with economic growth. There are 2,500 underworld groups in Japan with over 100,000 members and operating in

70% of the cities. Seven large syndicates dominate underworld crime and control approximately one-third of all gangs, known as *yakuza*. The largest of the gangs, Yamaguchigumi, has over 10,000 members in 34 prefectures. Gangsters style themselves as the inheritors of the samurai traditions and maintain a closely knit relationship. Nearly 10% of all people arrested and 50% of those arrested for drug smuggling, intimidation, extortion or gambling are underworld figures. Since the early 1980s they have given rise to a new type of crime, *sokaiya*, in which extortionists buy a small share of company stocks and then are paid by the companies either to manipulate stockholder meetings or to intimidate others from exposing company secrets or after-hours transgressions of its employees.

The percentage of crimes committed by the *burakumin* is higher than the national average. They have a higher rate of juvenile delinquency and are uncooperative toward and suspicious of the police.

HEALTH

Japan's extraordinary progress in health care is reflected in the rise in average life expectancy in 1985 to 74.84 years for males and to 80.46 years for females, among the highest in the world. With more people living longer, in 1985 the proportion of the elderly (over 65) exceeded 10% for the first time, reaching 10.3%. By 2000 this population will be 16.3%, and by 2021 one in four persons will be over 65. Japan then will have the oldest population in the world. The death rate has been declining correspondingly. Tuberculosis, once a major cause of death, has been superseded in this category by diseases characteristic of urban, industrialized societies—cerebral hemorrhage, cancer and heart disease. Particularly notable is the sharp decline in infant mortality, which declined from 60.1 per 1,000 births in 1950 to 7.5 per 1,000 births in 1980. Japan has been relatively unaffected by AIDS; only 59 cases of it were reported up to 1987.

HEALTH INDICATORS 1987

Health personnel
  Physicians: 161,101
    Person per physician: 663
  Dentists: 63,145
  Nurses: 595,091
  Pharmacists: 129,700
  Midwives: 24,649

```
┌─────────────────────────────────────────────────────┐
│          HEALTH INDICATORS 1987 (continued)           │
│ Hospitals                                             │
│   Number: 9,608                                       │
│   Number of beds: 1,495,000                           │
│     Per 10,000: 123                                   │
│   Admissions/discharges per 10,000: 643               │
│   Bed occupancy rate: 83.3                            │
│   Average length of stay: 56 days                     │
│                                                       │
│ Type of hospitals                                     │
│   Government: 15.8                                     │
│   Private nonprofit: 3.1                              │
│   Private profit: 81.1                                │
│                                                       │
│ Public health expenditures                            │
│   As % of national budget: N.A.                       │
│   Per capita: $472.20                                 │
│                                                       │
│ Vital statistics                                      │
│   Crude death rate per 1,000: 6.2                     │
│   Decline in death rate, 1965–84: -2.8                │
│   Life expectancy at birth (years)                    │
│     Males: 75.1                                       │
│     Females: 80.8                                     │
│   Infant mortality rate per 1,000 live births: 5.3    │
│   Child mortality rate ages 1–4 years per 1,000:      │
│     (.) insignificant                                 │
│   Maternal mortality rate per 100,000 live births: 15.3│
│ Causes of death per 100,000:                          │
│ Infectious & parasitic diseases: 9.6                  │
│ Cancer: 155.5                                         │
│ Endocrine & metabolic disorders: 9.1                  │
│ Diseases of the nervous system: 5.2                   │
│ Diseases of the circulatory system: 245.5             │
│ Diseases of the respiratory system: 80.3              │
│ Diseases of the digestive system: 31.5                │
│ Accidents, poisoning and violence: 46.7               │
└─────────────────────────────────────────────────────┘
```

The nation's medical bill in 1985 increased to Y16 trillion, attesting to the substantial investment in health care. One-quarter of the medical bill is accounted for by the elderly. Over half the hospitalized elderly were in the hospital for six months or longer, indicating the limited availability of home care and nursing services. Based on the number of doctors, dentists and nurses per capita, Japanese medical standards have reached Western levels. Medical services are being constantly expanded. In 1982 the government established 855 health centers throughout the country. During the 1980s the number of hospitals has risen by about 10% and that of hospital beds by 2.5%. The Medical Care Act was amended in 1974 to coordinate the health-care delivery functions of the prefectures and to establish a comprehensive and integrated system covering sickness prevention, diagnosis, treatment and rehabilitation.

FOOD & NUTRITION

Since the end of World War II, Japanese dietary patterns have changed radically and now resemble those of the West. For example, more Japanese now have toast and coffee for breakfast, although the older folks still prefer the traditional dishes with boiled rice, soybean paste soup and pickled vegetables. Consumption of cereals has diminished while that of milk, meat and dairy products has risen. With better living standards, the diet has become more nutritional. Average intake per day is 2,084 calories and 77.9 g. (2.7 oz.) of protein. Of the total protein intake, 26.5% comes from cereals (including 18.4% from rice), 9.6% from pulses, 23.1% from fish, 14.8% from livestock products, 11.0% from eggs and milk and 15% from other sources. However, most foodstuffs cost two to three times more in Japan than in the United States.

MEDIA & CULTURE

The Japanese press is relatively young. The first newspaper, *Batavia Shimbun* (a duplicate of an Indonesian Dutch publication), was published only in 1861. Technically, Japan was ready for the print media as early as the late 16th century, when printing from movable type was introduced almost simultaneously by Portuguese missionaries and the Japanese military—the latter learning of it from Korea. But before newspapers could evolve, the Tokugawa regime closed Japan's doors for about two centuries. The dawn of Meiji journalism saw two types of newspapers: *ko-shimbun* (small newspaper) and *oh-shimbun* (big newspaper). The former were mass-oriented and the latter elite papers. By the end of the 19th century, the *oh-shimbun* turned into political newspapers, many of them supported by the government and circumscribed by its regulations. Two of the modern giants were founded during that period: *Asahi Shimbun* in 1879 and *Mainichi Shimbun* in 1888. The Japanese military adventures in Asia in the early decades of the 20th century helped boost newspaper circulation. By 1924 *Mainichi Shimbun* had attained a phenomenal circulation of 1 million copies. The third contemporary giant, *Yomiuri Shimbun*, founded in 1874, began its rise soon after the great earthquake of 1923 by using some of William Randolph Hearst's techniques.

At the beginning of World War II a total of 1,422 newspapers were published in Japan, all of them subject to rigorous regimentation and thought-control regulation by the Showa government. The Domei News Agency was one of the largest in the world, with a staff of 3,000 and over 50 bureaus. Government dis-

PER CAPITA CONSUMPTION OF FOODS 1986
(kg/lb; lit/pint)

Potatoes: 35.1 kg. (77.3 lb.)
Wheat: 43.5 kg. (95.9 lb.)
Rice:
Fresh vegetables:
Fruits (total):
  Citrus:
  Noncitrus:
Eggs: 17.6 kg. (38.8 lb.)
Honey: 0.1 kg. (0.2 lb.)
Fish:
Milk: 36.4 kg. (80.2 lb.)
Butter: 0.7 kg. (1.5 lb.)
Cream:
Cheese: 0.8 kg. (1.6 lb.)
Yogurt:
Meat (total):
  Beef & veal: 6.2 kg. (13.6 lb.)
  Pig meat: 14.2 kg. (31.3 lb.)
  Poultry: 11.7 kg. (25.8 lb.)
  Mutton, lamb and goat:
Sugar: 23.0 kg. (50.7 lb.)
Chocolate:
Ice cream:
Margarine:
Biscuits:
Breakfast cereals:
Pasta:
Frozen foods:
Canned foods:
Beer: 41.3 l. (87.3 qt.)
Wine: 0.6 l. (1.1 qt.)
Alcoholic liquors: 2.4 l. (5.3 qt.)
Soft drinks: 65.0 l. (143.3 qt.)
Mineral waters:
Fruit juices:
Tea:
Coffee:
Cocoa:

pleasure with the press led to the passage of the National Mobilization Law of 1938, forcing the newspapers to merge and limiting one newspaper to a prefecture (for a total of 54). Severe censorship and government control of newsprint allocation added to the press's problems.

Press freedom returned to Japan with the nation's defeat and the beginning of the Occupation. One of the first acts of the supreme commander of Allied Powers (SCAP) was the abolition of all restrictive media legislation. However, in the effort to rid the press of all prewar influences, SCAP took some harsh measures. In the "red purge," all Communist as well as fascist editors and publishers were removed, and limited censorship was imposed on politically undesirable media. The structure of the industry also changed, as few newspapers were able to survive the economic consequences of the new order. Thus a pattern of monopoly and concentration began that has persisted to this day.

Japan leads the world in newspaper circulation per 1,000 and is second only to the Soviet Union in aggregate circulation. Morning editions are nearly twice as popular as evening editions; nearly 92% of these copies reach subscribers via delivery people, while 7.5% are sold at newsstands and 0.5% by other means, including mail. Among general newspapers, 99% of the copies are delivered to subscribers' homes. Japan has an elaborate delivery system, made up of over 23,000 circulation agents and 400,000 route employees. Trucks transport the bulk of the copies to the agents.

The rapid growth of the Japanese press is closely related to such national traits as intense curiosity, acquisitiveness and competitiveness. Japan's economic affluence and linguistic homogeneity also are positive factors. English is the only language other than Japanese in the print media. There are four English-language newspapers: *Japan Times*, *Mainichi Daily News*, *Daily Yomiuri* and *Asahi Evening News*. They are used by many Japanese readers to learn English-language skills or to upgrade them.

Only one Japanese newspaper—*Asahi Shimbun*—appears in John Merrill and Harold Fisher's *World's Great Newspapers*, but most Japanese newspapers consider themselves to be quality newspapers. The press has a good reputation for good professional reporting of national and international events. International news receives prominent treatment because of traditional Japanese interest in foreign developments affecting their own economy. Well into the 1970s, the press had been accused of being docile toward the government and of lacking individuality. The tradition of an adversary press had never flourished in Japan for historical reasons and, further, the government was not above buying special favors from publishers by giving tax exemptions and subsidies. Some of the blame for the lack of variety was attributed to the *kisha* (reporters') clubs common to Japan; these clubs exercised exclusive rights over news sources and barred nonestablishment journalists. Investigative and adversarial reporting began in the late 1970s and became a standard feature among the large dailies in the 1980s. For the first time bylines appeared, making reporters accountable for what they wrote. Journalists also became more aggressive in following up news, relying less on government handouts.

Economically the Japanese press is one of the most prosperous in the world, sharing the general dynamism of the nation. Such prosperity represented a turnaround from the near-depression in the industry that characterized the 1970s. In 1976 *Mainichi Shimbun* was close to bankruptcy, while others were reducing their work force and number of pages. The industry was saved by a surge in advertising revenues and the introduction of labor-saving technologies. Since 1962 Japanese newspapers have received more income from ads than from sales. Among the major newspapers ads take up between 40% and 45% of space.

The chief characteristic of the Japanese press, besides its size, is its tendency toward concentration. This is evident from the fact that Japan's huge aggregate circulation of 68 million copies (larger than the rest of Asia combined!) is concentrated in 126 dailies. The top five of these newspapers account for about 60%. *Yomiuri Shimbun* is the second-largest-selling newspaper in the world, next to *Pravda.* The top five having printing plants in every region and publish more than 120 regional editions. Concentration and, in some cases, monopoly, is common in the local press. In most prefectures, only one newspaper is published, continuing the World War II tradition. Such a monopoly gives the local press a strong economic foundation. Some local newspapers are so profitable that they have acquired newspaper properties outside the home prefectures, thus becoming what are known as bloc newspapers.

LEADING NEWSPAPERS OF JAPAN-1986	
Newspaper	Circulation
Yomiuri Shimbun	8,974,000
Asahi Shimbun	7,471,000
Mainichi Shimbun	4,187,000
Nihon Keizai Shimbun	1,370,000
Chunichi Shimbun	1,980,000
Hokkaido Shimbun	1,100,000

Press concentration also is prevalent in ownership structure. Most newspapers are closely held corporations. The top newspapers, such as *Yomiuri Shimbun, Asahi Shimbun, Mainichi Shimbun* and *Nihon Keizai Shimbun,* are 100% owned by their family owners, while another 24 newspapers have 50% or more of their ownership in the hands of families or employees.

Japan is the third-largest newsprint producer in the world and the second-largest newsprint consumer. Consumption is large because of high advertising volume. Since 1980 Japan has produced lightweight newsprint.

Japan has been unique among industrialized nations in its ability to introduce new production systems with virtually no interference from labor unions. Japanese unions were not hostile during the technological upgrading because they did not face personnel dismissals and were assured of continuous employment.

Because of intense company loyalty—reinforced by stock ownership—strikes are rare, and when workers strike, they do so after working hours. Reductions in personnel strength have been achieved mainly through hiring freezes. As a result, the average age of newspaper employees is much higher today than it was about 25 years ago.

Freedom of the press is built into the 1947 Constitutions as one of its bulwarks and has never been seriously challenged in postwar history. Occasional infringements have arisen from other legal provisions, such as invasion of privacy, obscenity, official secrets and nondisclosure of news sources. Provisions regarding obscenity, formerly strict, have been gradually relaxed during the late 1970s and 1980s. Generally, court rulings have been in favor of the press functioning without trammels. However, there are a number of self-imposed limitations, among them the three so-called institutional inhibitions: criticism of the royal family, exposure of right-wing gangsters and corrupt politicians, and the burakumin. Being generally proestablishment, the press has a tendency to cover up ugly stories that may discredit establishment figures and institutions. During the scandal that led to the fall of Prime Minister Tanaka, the press as a whole suppressed the story until overtaken by events.

MEDIA INDICATORS 1986

Newspapers
Number of dailies: 124
Circulation (000): 68,653
Per 1,000: 569

Number of nondailies: N.A.
Circulation (000):
Per capita:

Number of periodicals: 2,138
Circulation: 36,293,000

Newsprint consumption
Total: 2,736,800 tons
Per capita: 23 kg (50.7 lb.)

Book publishing
Number of titles: 44,253

Broadcasting
Annual expenditures: Yen 1.332 trillion
Number of employees: 42,078

Radio
Number of transmitters: 1,070
Number of radio receivers: 95 million
    Persons per receiver: 1.3
Annual total program hours: 497,351

MEDIA INDICATORS 1986 *(continued)*

Television
  Television transmitters: 12,756
  Number of TV receivers: 30.250 million
    Persons per receiver: 4
  Annual total program hours: 667,761

Cinema
  Number of fixed cinemas: 2,137
  Seating capacity: 918,000
    Seats per 1,000: 7.8
  Annual attendance (million): 155 per capita: 1.3
  Gross box office receipts: Yen 163.529 billion

Films
  Production of long films: 319
  Import of long films: 199
    3.5% from United Kingdom
    8.8% from Italy
    10.6% from France
    58.3% from United States

CULTURAL & ENVIRONMENTAL INDICATORS 1986

Public libraries
  Number: 1,028
  Volumes: 97,172,000
  Registered borrowers: 10,947,000
  Loans per 1,000: 1,579

Museums: 571
  Annual attendance: 57,386,000
  Attendance per 1,000: 480

Performing arts facilities: 140
  Number of performances: 39,768
  Annual attendance: N.A.
  Attendance per 1,000: N.A.

Ecological sites
  Number of facilities: 50
  Botanical gardens and zoos: 105

Japan has two main news agencies, both born out of the wartime Domei. The Kyodo News Service, formed in 1945, is a nonprofit organization similar to the Associated Press, while the Jiji Press, also formed in 1945, plays a role similar to that of UPI. Both news agencies are very strong in foreign reporting, with over 431 correspondents in virtually all major cities.

Broadcasting has both commercial and noncommercial sectors. Nippon Hoso Kyokai (NHK), the only noncommercial broadcaster, operates two television and three radio networks and two DBS television services. Overall, NHK has 6,914 television stations (3,010 educational), 326 AM radio stations, one shortwave radio station and 503 FM radio stations. The commercial sector includes 103 television companies and 34 radio companies with 6,262 television stations, 93 FM radio stations, 208 AM radio stations and two shortwave radio stations.

SOCIAL WELFARE

Social Security programs are administered by the Ministry of Health and Welfare at the central level and by the municipal and prefectural governments at the local level. Japan's Social Security programs are basically a combination of income security provided through social insurance and public welfare assistance; medical care security through health insurance; and social welfare service, including care of children, the physically and mentally handicapped and the aged. Total annual social welfare expenditures represent 12.7% of the GNP. Cash benefits surpassed medical care benefits for the first time in 1975, indicating the changing structure of the Social Security System. The weight of pensions has shown an upward tendency, while medical care insurance has shown a downward trend.

In Japan, the elderly segment of the population still is smaller than that in many Western countries, and the social benefits extended to this sector are correspondingly less. But the population is aging faster than those in the United States and Europe, so that by the first decades of the 21st century there will be a substantial rise in payments both for pensions and medical care in Japan.

As a result of many factors, such as the Japanese employment system, with its lifelong employment and seniority wage features, coupled with a stronger emphasis on personal and human relations, nonobligatory welfare programs undertaken by companies and institutions over and above their legal obligations are quite extensive. Life insurance and retirement benefits help to cushion the economic consequences of aging. Family solidarity still is strong in Japan and adds a measure of stability to the lives of older people. For instance, it still is usual for old folks to live with their children. Even when parents live separately, children can be counted on to provide basic amenities and thus reduce dependence on the impersonal services of the state. To encourage these traditional family support systems, the government extends tax concessions for care of the elderly.

Social insurance is divided into occupational insurance for public and private employees and community insurance for others, including the self-employed. There are eight public pension plans of different vintage, some dating from the late 1800s. These eight are being consolidated into a basic pension system applicable to all over a certain age.

Since 1961 all Japanese have been covered under some kind of health insurance program, which provides medical treatment (free of charge or with the payment of a small fee) in addition to various health-related allowances. The present system consists of three different plans. First, there is employee insurance under the aegis of the government or a health insurance society. Second, there are health insurance plans for employees in particular fields of work, such as seamen and teachers. National Health Insurance is a community health insurance program for those not covered by the above two plans. It is managed either by local authorities or the National Health Insurance Association. The benefit rates for employees' health insurance are 90% for the insured (10% to be paid by the patient) and 70% (30% to be paid by the insured) for family dependents. In National Health Insurance the benefit rate is 70% for both the insured and family dependents. Cash benefits include sickness and injury allowances; maternity allowances; and lump-sum payments covering childbirth, nursing and funerals. The costs of National Health Insurance are covered mainly by premiums and subsidies from the national treasury. Some local governments levy an insurance tax, varying according to income, assets and number of members in each household.

Income security programs consist mainly of old-age, survivors and disability pension plans, which fall under various social insurance programs as well as unemployment insurance and workmen's accident compensation insurance, both of which are administered separately. Pension plans cover employees in general (Employees' Pension Insurance) and particular occupational groups, besides a community plan for nonemployees, called National Pension Insurance. These plans vary in the starting age for benefit payment, premium levels and the method for calculating the amount of pension. For example, National Pension Insurance is based on fixed formula providing for a uniform pension. The Mutual Aid Association's pension is proportional to the remuneration of the insured portion, and these two methods are mixed in the Employees' Pension Insurance so that a pensioner with 28 years of coverage receives 60% of his average standard remuneration, excluding bonuses. The elderly over 70, widows with children and the disabled who are not covered by any contributory pension plan have been entitled since 1959 to receive benefits under a noncontributory welfare pension plan paid out of the national budget.

Public assistance programs provide assistance to the indigent in seven areas: daily necessities, medical expenses, children's education, housing, maternity, occupational training and funeral services. A total of 80% of the cost of these programs is met by the central government and 20% by local governments. Less than 1.2% of the population receive such assistance.

Welfare facilities and services are offered by national and local governments and private social welfare bodies. These are available to the handicapped, the elderly, and children with special problems. Many of these services are being offered at home through what are known as "silver services." These domiciliary services are expected to grow much faster than institutional services.

CHRONOLOGY (from 1945)

1945—Japan signs surrender. . . . The Occupation of Japan begins under the supreme commander of Allied Powers (SCAP), General of the Army Douglas MacArthur. . . . A new cabinet is formed under Kijuro Shidehara.

1946—SCAP completes demobilization and demiliatrization and embarks on extensive civil reforms, including land reform, and the dissolution of *zaibatsu*. . . . Hirohito formally renounces divinity. . . . Liberal Party forms first government under Shigeru Yoshida.

1947—New Constitution replaces the Meiji Constitution and includes provision renouncing war. . . . New Police Law creates a decentralized police administration under the National Public Safety Commission. . . . Socialists under Tetsu Katayama form first ministry under new Constitution.

1948—War Crimes Tribunal set up under the Postdam Declaration; 25 war criminals are sentenced to death or life imprisonment and 202,000 are debarred from public life. . . . Hitoshi Ashida serves for eight months as Democratic Party prime minister, followed by Liberal Party's Shigeru Yoshida.

1951—San Francisco Peace Conference negotiates a treaty of peace with Japan, ending state of war and Occupation and restoring full sovereignty to Japan by April 1952.

1952—Japan and the United States sign security treaty. . . . The National Police Reserve is transformed into the National Safety Forces, which later became the Self-Defense Forces.

1954—Ichiro Hatoyama of the Democratic Party replaces Yoshida as prime minister.

1955—Japan's socialist parties unite to form the Japan Socialist Party, and the Liberal Party and the Democratic Party merge to form the Liberal Democratic Party.

1956—Tanzan Ishibashi begins a two-month term as prime minister. . . . Japan is admitted to the United Nations and establishes diplomatic relations with the Soviet Union.

1957—Nobusuke Nishi begins a three-year term in office as prime minister.

1960—Hayato Ikeda begins a four-year term in office as prime minister.

1964—Eisaku Sato, brother of Nishi, begins eight-year term as prime minister.

1970—United States returns Okinawa and Ryukyu Islands to Japan.

1972—Sato yields office to Kakuei Tanaka, who heads government for the next two years.

1974—Tanaka is implicated in the Lockheed scandal, is arrested for receiving a bribe of Y500 million and is forced to step down in favor of Takeo Miki.

1976—Takeo Fukuda begins a two-year tenure as prime minister.

1978—Masayoshi Ohira begins a two-year term as prime minister.

1980—Zenko Suzuki begins a two-year term as prime minister.

1982—Yasuhiro Nakasone begins a five-year term as prime minister.

1987—Noboru Takeshita replaces Nakasone as prime minister.

1989—Implicated in an influence-peddling scandal, Takeshita steps down and is replaced by Sosuke Uno; Uno is forced to resign in the wake of a sex scandal and Toshiki Kaifu is named premier.

BIBLIOGRAPHY

BOOKS

Allen, G. C. *Japanese Economy*. New York, 1982.

———. *A Short Economic History of Modern Japan*. New York, 1980.

———. *Japan's Economic Expansion*. London, 1965.

Austin, Lewis. *Japan: The Paradox of Progress*. New Haven, Conn., 1976.

Baerwald, Hans. *Japan's Parliament*. New York, 1974.

Beasley, William G. *The Modern History of Japan*. New York, 1974.

Benedict, Ruth. *The Chrysanthemum and the Sword*. New York, 1967.

Benjamin, Roger, and Kan Ori. *Tradition and Change in Postindustrial Japan: The Role of Political Parties*. New York, 1981.

Bieda, K. *Structure and Operation of the Japanese Economy*. New York, 1982.

Blotho, Andrea. *Japan: An Economic Survey, 1953–73*. New York, 1975.

Borton, Hugh. *Japan's Modern Century*. New York, 1971.

Brzezinski, Zbigniew K. *The Fragile Blossom: Crisis and Change in Japan*. New York, 1971.

Buck, James H. *The Modern Japanese Military System*. Beverly Hills, Calif., 1975.

Burks, Ardath. *Government of Japan*. Westport, Conn., 1982.

———. *Japan: Profile of a Postindustrial Power*. Boulder, Colo., 1984.

Campbell, John C. *Contemporary Japanese Budgetary Politics*. Berkeley, Calif., 1977.

Chapman, J. W., and R. Drifte. *Japan's Quest for Comprehensive Security: Defense, Diplomacy and Dependence*. New York, 1983.

Christopher, Robert C. *The Japanese Mind: The Goliath Explained.* New York, 1984.

Clark, Rodney. *The Japanese Company.* New Haven, Conn., 1979.

Craig, Albert M. *Japan: A Comparative View.* Princeton, N.J., 1979.

Denison, Edward F., and William K. Chung. *How Japan's Economy Grew So Fast: The Sources of Postwar Expansion.* Washington, D.C., 1976.

DeVoss, George. *Institutions for Change in Japanese Society.* Berkeley, Calif., 1984.

Dore, Ronald R. *Aspects of Social Change in Modern Japan.* Princeton, N.J., 1967.

Duus, Peter. *The Rise of Modern Japan.* Boston, 1976.

Frank, Isaiah. *The Japanese Economy in International Perspective.* Baltimore, 1975.

Fukui, Eiichir. *The Climate of Japan.* New York, 1977.

Fukuii, Haruhiro. *Parties in Power: The Japanese Liberal Democrats and Policy making.* Berkeley, Calif. 1970.

Fukutake, Tadashi. *Japanese Society Today.* New York, 1981.

———. *Japanese Social Structure.* New York, 1982.

Gibney, Frank. *Japan: The Fragile Superpower.* New York, 1985.

———. *Miracle by Design: The Real Reasons Behind Japan's Economic Success.* New York, 1982.

Grossberg, Kenneth A. *Japan Today.* Philadelphia, 1981.

Guillain, Robert. *The Japanese Challenge.* New York, 1970.

Haitani, Kanji. *The Japanese Economic System: An Institutional Approach.* Lexington, Mass., 1976.

Hall, John W. *Japan.* New York, 1971.

Halliday, Jon. *A Political History of Japanese Capitalism.* New York, 1975.

Hanami, Tadashi. *Labor Relations in Japan Today.* New York, 1982.

Hane, Mikiso. *Japan: A Historical Survey.* New York, 1972.

Hidaka, Rokuro. *The Price of Affluence: Dilemmas of Contemporary Japan.* New York, 1984.

Hillman, Donald. *Japanese-American Relations.* Washington, D.C., 1985.

Hirscheier, Johannes, and Tsunehiko Yui. *The Development of Japanese Business.* London, 1981.

Holland, Harrison M. *Managing Diplomacy: The United States and Japan.* Stanford, Calif., 1985.

Horne, James. *Japan's Financial Markets: Conflict and Consensus in Policymaking.* London, 1985.

Ichino, Tatsuro. *Japan's Postwar Economy.* New York, 1983.

Ike, Nobutaka. *Japanese Politics: Patron-Client Democracy.* New York, 1972.

————. *Japan: The New Superstate.* San Francisco, 1974.

Ishida, R. *Geography of Japan.* Tokyo, 1961.

Ishida, Takeshi. *Japanese Political Culture: Change and Continuity.* New Brunswick, N.J., 1983.

Ishii, Ryosuke. *A History of Political Institutions in Japan.* New York, 1980.

Jansen, Maurice B. *Changing Japanese Attitudes Toward Modernization.* Princeton, N.J., 1965.

Kajima, Morinasuke. *The Emergence of Japan as a World Power, 1895–1925.* Rutland, Vt., 1968.

————. *Modern Japan's Foreign Policy.* Rutland, Vt., 1969.

Katz, Joshua D. *Japan's New World Role.* Boulder, Colo., 1985.

Kawai, Kazuo. *Japan's American Interlude.* Chicago, 1960.

Kobayashi, M. *Japan: The Most Misunderstood Country.* New York, 1984.

Kodansha Encyclopedia of Japan, nine vols. New York, 1983.

Kojima K., and T. Ozawa. *Japan's General Trading Companies.* Washington, D.C., 1985.

Kosai, Yutaka. *The Era of High-Speed Growth: Notes of the Modern Japanese Economy.* New York, 1984.

———— and Yoshitaro Ogino. *Contemporary Japanese Economy.* White Plains, N.Y., 1984.

Kosaka, Masataka. *One Hundred Million Japanese.* New York, 1972.

Kunio, Yoshihara. *Sogo Shosha: The Vanguard of Japanese Economy.* New York, 1982.

Langdon, Frank C. *Japan's Foreign Policy.* Vancouver, B.C., 1973.

Langer, Paul F. *Communism in Japan.* Stanford, Calif., 1972.

Lebra, Joyce, et al. *Women in Changing Japan.* Stanford, Calif., 1976.

Lincoln, Edward J. *Japan: Facing Economic Maturity.* Washington, D.C., 1986.

Lockwood, William W. *The State and Economic Enterprise in Japan.* Princeton, N.J., 1965.

————. *Economic Development in Japan.* Princeton, N.J., 1970.

Magaziner, Ira C., and Thomas M. Hout. *Japanese Industrial Policy.* Berkeley, Calif., 1981.

Maki, John M. *Government and Politics in Japan.* New York, 1978.

Mason, Richard H., and John G. Caiger. *A History of Japan.* New York, 1973.

McNelly, Theodore. *Politics and Government in Japan.* Lanham, Md., 1985.

Mendl, Wolf. *Western Europe and Japan Between the Superpowers.* New York, 1984.

Morishima, M. *Why Has Japan Succeeded? Western Technology and the Japanese Ethos.* New York, 1982.

Murata, Kiyoji, and Ota Isamu. *An Industrial Geography of Japan.* New York, 1980.

Najita, Tetsuo. *Japan.* Englewood Cliffs, N.J., 1972.

———. *Japan: The Intellectual Foundation of Modern Politics.* Chicago, 1980.

Nakamura, Takafusa. *The Postwar Japanese Economy: Its Development and Structure.* New York, 1981.

Nakane, Chie. *Japanese Society.* Berkeley, Calif., 1972.

Nobuya, Shikaumi. *Cultural Policy in Japan.* Paris, 1970.

Norbeck, Edward. *Changing Japan.* Prospect Heights, Ill., 1984.

Norman, E. H. *Japan's Emergence as a Modern State.* New York, 1946.

Oestler, I. M. *Managing an Alliance: The Politics of U.S.-Japanese Relations.* Washington, D.C., 1976.

Ohhkawa, Kazushi. *Patterns of Japanese Economic Development.* New Haven, Conn., 1979.

———. *Japanese Economic Growth.* Stanford, Calif., 1973.

——— and Gustav Ranis. *Japan and the Developing Countries.* Oxford, 1985.

Okimoto, Daniel I. *Japan's Economy: Coping with Change in the International Environment.* Boulder, Colo., 1982.

Okita, Saburo. *The Developing Economics of Japan.* New York, 1981.

Olson, Lawrence. *Japan in Postwar Asia.* New York, 1970.

Ozaki, Robert S. *The Japanese: A Cultural Portrait.* Rutland, Vt., 1978.

——— and Walter Arnold. *Japan's Foreign Relations: A Global Search for Economic Security.* Boulder, Colo., 1984.

Papinot, E. *Historical and Geographical Dictionary of Japan.* Ruthland, Vt., 1972.

Passin, Herbert. *Society and Education in Japan.* New York, 1983.

——— and Gerald Curtis. *Japan in the Nineteen Eighties.* Atlanta, 1983.

Patrick, Hugh, and Henry Rosovsk. *Asia's New Giant: How the Japanese Economy Works.* Washington, D.C., 1978.

Pempel, T. J. *Policymaking in Contemporary Japan.* Ithaca, N.Y., 1977.

———. *Policy and Politics in Japan: Creative Conservatism.* Philadelphia, 1982.

Pezeu-Massabuau, Jacques. *The Japanese Islands: A Physical and Social Geography.* Rutland, Vt., 1978.

Reischauer, Edwin O. *Japan: Past and Present.* New York, 1956.

———. *United States and Japan.* Cambridge, Mass., 1965.

———. *The Japanese.* Cambridge, Mass., 1977.

———. *Japan: The Story of a Nation.* New York, 1970.

Richardson, Bradley. *The Political Culture of Japan.* Berkeley, Calif., 1974.

——— and Scott C. Flanagan. *Politics in Japan.* Boston, 1984.

Romuta, Kensaburo. *Japan's Economy in World Perspective*. Berkeley, Calif., 1983.

Ross, Joel, and William Ross. *Japanese Quality Circles and Productivity*. Englewood Cliffs, N.Y., 1982.

Sansom, Sir George Bailey. *A History of Japan*, three vols. Stanford, Calif., 1958–63.

———. Japan: A Short Cultural History. New York, 1962.

Sato, Kazuo. *Industry and Business in Japan*. White Plains, N.Y., 1980.

——— and Yasuo Hashino. *The Anatomy of Japanese Business*. White Plains, N.Y., 1984.

Scalapino, Robert A. *The Foreign Policy of Modern Japan*. Berkeley, Calif., 1977.

Seward, Jack. *More About the Japanese*. Rutland, Vt., 1983.

Shibusawa, Masanide. *Japan and the Asia-Pacific Region: Profile of Change*. New York, 1985.

Shinohara, Miyohei. *Industrial Development, Trade and Business Cycles in Japan*. New York, 1982.

Shiratori, Rei. *Japan in the Nineteen Eighties*. New York, 1983.

———. *Japan Today*. Manchester, 1984.

Shively, Donald H. *Tradition and Modernization in Japanese Culture*. Princeton, N.Y., 1971.

Steiner, Kurt. *Local Government in Japan*. Stanford, Calif., 1965.

Stockwin, J. A. *Japan: Divided Politics in a Growth Economy*. New York, 1982.

Storry, Richard. *A History of Modern Japan*. New York, 1960.

Taira, Koji. *Economic Development and the Labor Market in Japan*. New York, 1970.

Takamiya, Susumu, and Keith Thurley. *Japan's Emerging Multinationals*. New York, 1982.

Thayer, Nathaniel B. *How the Conservatives Rule Japan*. Princeton, 1969.

Thomas, Roy. *Japan: The Growth of an Industrial Power*. Toronto, 1971.

Tiedemann, Arthur E. *An Introduction to Japanese Civilization*. New York, 1974.

Toland, John. *The Rising Sun*. New York, 1971.

Trevor, Malcolm. *Japan's Reluctant Multinationals*. New York, 1983.

Tsunoda, Ryusaku. *Sources of Japanese Tradition*. New York, 1958.

Tung, Rosalie L. *Key to Japan's Economic Strength: Human Potential*. Lexington, Ky., 1984.

Varley, Paul H. *Japanese Culture: A Short History*. New York, 1973.

Ward, Robert E. *Political Development in Modern Japan*. Princeton, N.J., 1968.

———. *Japan's Political System*. Englewood Cliffs, N.J., 1978.

Watanuki, Joji. *Politics in Postwar Japanese Society.* New York, 1977.

Webb, Herschel. *Japan Emerges.* New York, 1974.

———. *An Introduction to Japan.* New York, 1957.

Woronoff, Jon. *Inside Japan, Inc.* Rutland, Vt., 1982.

———. *Japan's Commercial Empire.* White Plains, N.Y., 1984.

Yanaga, Chitoshi. *Big Business in Japanese Politics.* New Haven, Conn., 1971.

STATISTICAL SOURCES

The statistical data used in the book are derived from a number of sources, most of them published by international organizations.

(Annuals unless otherwise noted)

Banks, Arthur. *Cross National Time Series.* Binghamton, N.Y.

Central Intelligence Agency. *World Factbook.* Washington, D.C.

Energy Information Administration. *International Energy Annual.* Washington, D.C.

Euromonitor Publications. *European Marketing Data and Statistics.* London.

———. *International Marketing Data and Statistics.* London.

Food and Agriculture Organization. *Production Yearbook.* Rome.

———. *Trade Yearbook.* Rome.

———. *Yearbook of Fishery Statistics.* Rome.

———. *Yearbook of Forest Products.* Rome.

Institute for Strategic Studies. *The Military Balance.* London.

International Civil Aviation Organization. *Digest of Statistics-Airline Traffic.* Montreal.

International Labor Office. *Yearbook of Labor Statistics.* Geneva.

International Monetary Fund. *Balance of Payments Yearbook.* Washington, D.C.

———. *Direction of Trade Statistics.* Washington, D.C.

———. *International Financial Statistics.* Washington, D.C.

International Road Federation. *World Road Statistics.* Washington, D.C.

International Telecommunications Union. *Telecommunications Statistics.* Geneva.

INTERPOL. *International Crime Statistics.* Paris, biennial.

OECD. *OECD Economic Outlook.* Paris, periodical.

———. *OECD Financial Market Trends and OECD Financial Statistics.* Paris, periodical.

———. *Indicators of Industrial Activity.* Paris, periodical.

———. *Main Economic Indicators.* Paris, periodical.

———. *Main Science and Technology Indicators.* Paris, periodical.

———. *OECD Observer.* Paris, periodical.

————. *OECD Economic Surveys.* Paris, occasional.

————. *OECD Economic Outlook.* Paris, periodical.

————. *OECD Economic Studies.* Paris, periodical.

————. *Quarterly Labor Force Statistics.* Paris, periodical.

————. *Quarterly National Accounts.* Paris, periodical.

————. *Quarterly Oil Statistics and Energy Balances.* Paris, periodical.

————. *Monthly Statistics of Foreign Trade.* Paris, periodical.

————. *Reviews of National Policies for Education.* Paris, series.

————. *National Policies and Agricultural Trade.* Paris, series.

————. *Competition Policy in OECD Countries.* Paris, series.

————. *Consumer Policy in OECD Countries.* Paris, series.

————. *Revenue Statistics of OECD Countries.* Paris, series.

————. *Trends in Banking Structure and Regulation in OECD Countries.* Paris, series.

————. *Information, Computer, and Communications Policy.* Paris, series.

————. *Reviews of National Science Policy.* Paris, series.

————. *Innovation Policy.* Paris, series.

————. *Industrial Structure Statistics.* Paris.

————. *Labour Force Statistics.* Paris.

————. *OECD Employment Outlook.* Paris.

————. *Energy Balances of OECD Countries.* Paris.

————. *Energy Statistics.* Paris.

————. *National Accounts of OECD Countries.* Paris.

Sivard, Ruth Leger. *World Military & Social Expenditures.* Leesburg, VA.

United Nations. *Demographic Yearbook.* New York.

————. *Monthly Bulletin of Statistics.* New York.

————. *Population and Vital Statistical Report.* New York, monthly.

————. *Statistical Yearbook.* New York.

————. *Yearbook of Industrial Statistics.* New York.

————. *Yearbook of International Trade Statistics.* New York.

————. *Yearbook of National Accounts Statistics.* New York.

————. *Yearbook of World Energy Statistics.* New York.

UNCTAD. *Handbook of International Trade and Development Statistics.* Geneva.

UNESCO. *Statistical Yearbook.* Paris.

U.S. Bureau of Mines. *Minerals Yearbook.* Washington, D.C.

U.S. Arms Control and Disarmament Agency. *Worldwide Military Expenditures and Related Data.* Washington, D.C.

U.S. G.P.O. *Social Security Systems of the World.* Washington, D.C., occasional.

World Bank. *World Bank Atlas*. Washington, D.C.
———. *World Development Report*. Washington, D.C.
WHO. *World Health Statistics Annual*. Geneva.
World Tourism Organization. *World Travel Statistics*. Madrid.

INDEX